RAISING ME:

A Story of God's Redemptive Grace and Power

By Lori H. Huggins

RAISING ME:

A Story of God's Redemptive Grace and Power

Copyright ©2021 by Lori H. Huggins

Printed in the United States of America
ISBN #978-1-7357752-7-2

All rights are reserved solely by the author.
The author declares that the contents are original and
do not infringe on the rights of any other person.

No part of this book may be reproduced in any form except with
permission from the author. The views in this book are not necessarily
the views of the publisher.

Contents

1) The Journey .... Page 5

2) Born Again .... Page 13

3) The Regeneration .... Page 29

4) The Greatest Refuge .... Page 34

5) Afrocentric Liberation .... Page 42

6) This Can't Be Happening .... Page 56

7) Losing Home, Losing Her .... Page 69

8) Slander and Betrayal .... Page 78

9) The Fruits of Our Labor .... Page 99

10) The Rededication .... Page 107

11) Those Deep, Dark Family Secrets .... Page 110

12) What Is Love? .... Page 123

Introduction

Sometimes life seems to deal you a crummy deck of cards. As people always say, "when life gives you lemons, make lemonade." This saying is often true of those who have not yet experienced a "God encounter," which we know as the regeneration of the soul in Jesus Christ. Sometimes, in this world, we are given ideal settings and circumstances to grow and flow successfully. Everyone's story is different; in reality, there are no ideal circumstances. However, when you have something called faith, it can help you move mountains, which often turn out to be molehills when you understand the purpose of life's obstacles and challenges. We can complain, we can give up in the face of tragedy, and sometimes we have to cry, scream, yell, or vent to a best friend, pastor, or therapist. Through each trial and tribulation, we grow deeper roots in the soil of faith, like the tree planted by the water (Psalm 1:3). We may take detours or want to disconnect, but once we have tasted and seen that the Lord is good (Psalm 34:8), we understand the source of our strength.

We are indeed never alone, as the Psalmist said, "even when my mother and father forsake me, the Lord will lift me" (Psalm 27:10). We have an advocate in the Father (1 John 2:1), who is fighting for us amid betrayal, sickness, death, loss, divorce, depression, and joy. We can cry Abba, Father because He is our father (Romans 8:15). "The godly may trip seven times, but they will get up again. But one disaster is enough to overthrow the wicked" (Proverbs 24:16). Not only can Christ raise us spiritually from the dead, using the same power that raised Him physically, but God is a Father to the fatherless (Psalm 68:5) and a mother to the motherless. He is fully capable of raising and guiding His children into His will and along the path of righteousness if they say yes to His leadership. Hence, He has raised me and continues to raise me by "pulling me out of the muck and miry clay and planting my feet firmly on a rock to stay" (Psalm 40:2).

The Journey

I made my earthly debut on a windy, wintery evening during a *Jackson Five* concert at Radio City Music Hall in New York City. I know this because my wonderful, funny, witty Godfather was attending this concert, while his two best friends (who happened to be my parents) were in labor. My birth was difficult, according to my mother, and I had to be pulled out with forceps. Eventually, I emerged successfully from my mother's womb, with everything intact. However, thirteen months later, my mother noticed that I was not walking flat on my feet. She took me to various doctors and specialists, only to be told that her daughter might have cerebral palsy. She ran frantically around town, searching for a credible second opinion from some of the best medical professionals. One doctor finally simulated throwing me to the ground and observed the reflexes I used to prevent myself from falling. This test proved, beyond a shadow of a doubt, that I did NOT have cerebral palsy. To God be all the glory, all the honor, and all the praise!

As time passed, I began to walk with leg braces, which I hated because they were uncomfortable and confining. I also had to deal with people asking my mother questions about what was "wrong" with me. I used to hear my mother explaining to people in the community that I was a "toe walker," not some crippled child destined to wear strange footwear all my life. I could see my mother's frustration, even while she was trying to be pleasant, with a Hollywood smile on her face. Underneath, she wanted to tell people to mind their own business. She was a very prideful, dignified, and private woman, much like her mother, my grandmother. As time went on, God rectified the situation, and everyone was simply glad that I did not have a severe neurological disorder.

From the very beginning, my life seemed to follow a pattern of numerous roadblocks, with tremendous victories following after. Although there were always "struggles," I recognized that this was God's way of making me learn to rely on Him from an early stage. My parents first caught a glimpse of each other as teenagers in the Bronx at the Forest Houses, where my mother lived briefly after leaving Harlem. Both of them recalled seeing each other "around the way," but they never connected. Later, they were introduced in Evergreen Gardens in the Soundview section of the Bronx by James Ash, who later became my godfather and was the person at the Jackson Five concert on the night I was born. My parents became fast friends; they had both been mistreated in their first marriages. A year and a half later, my parents were living together and then got married. Lesson: A year and a half is not enough time for two people to heal from previous marriages where their spouses cheated on them both. My parents were young and naive.

The first challenge of my existence began with my conception, as my mother tried for almost four years to get pregnant with me. My mother's difficulties were so great that my father had a varicocelectomy to support her fertility since my mother had been on the pill for such a long time. What's that, you ask? A man has a varicocelectomy when he has a vein blockage in the testicular area that decreases the chance of egg fertilization, not enough sperm can make the journey to a woman's eggs. There you have it—and that's today's Biology 101 lesson! Anyway, this shows that even my conception was difficult, as was my actual birth, followed by my ability to crawl (my mother said I hopped) and walked.

The Forest Houses was a new housing project, and my parents met in passing a few times on the street. Both of them grew up in Harlem in New York City. My father was born in Harlem and lived there until the age of six. Then he was sent to his mother's hometown of Orangeburg, South Carolina, for two years. He returned to the Bronx when he was about eight years old. My mother was born in midtown Manhattan and brought home from the hospital to Harlem, where most of her family lived at that time. In the 1940s and 1950s, my mother lived in the Sugar Hill/Hamilton Heights section of Harlem near City College, a very elite address.

Many African American historical greats, including Count Bassie, Joe Louis, Lena Horne, Langston Hughes, Sidney Poitier, Billie Holiday, and Paul Robeson, lived in the Hamilton Heights section of Harlem.

My father's life was quite different from my mothers'. His mother came from South Carolina, while my maternal grandmother was born and raised in New York City by a West-Indian father and an African American mother. From the U.S. Census records, I learned that my mother's side became literate much earlier than my father's side, after slavery and the Jim Crow era. Socioeconomic class makes a huge difference in relationships. In hindsight, I can see that my father was exceptionally intelligent, as was his mother. However, culturally and socio-economically, my parents were vastly different.

My mother's side of the family was very upwardly mobile, without a trace of Southern dialect in their accents and speaking ways. Although they were not degreed Black people, many were "fair-skinned," articulate, and good at mingling with upper-class Black people and White folks because they were well-read. My mother's family mingled with Harlem's Delany's, who represented the real African American upper middle class. Harriet Delany, the niece of the famed Delany Sisters, was one of my grandmother's best friends and later married her first cousin. My father never knew his biological father. According to my paternal grandmother, my grandfather, Harold Johnson, came from a relatively middle-class background in Camden, South Carolina. I got the sense that my grandmother was considered to be not good enough for his family in 1943 after she became pregnant with her first-born son, my father. In those days, men were supposed to respect women's honor and marry them quickly if they became pregnant. Being an unwed mother devastated my grandmother and negatively impacted my father, which lasted throughout his entire life. My grandmother eventually married and had a second child by the time my father was nine years old. Still, his stepfather (who fathered one girl in this union) was abusive, alcoholic, and harmed the entire family. My paternal grandmother left this man, who later passed away. Sometime later, she met Mr. HC and had three more children with him in a common-law union. Despite growing up in a town outside Columbia, South Carolina, during segregation, she went on to become a graduate student at Columbia University, where she obtained her master's degree in teaching. In her late forties, my paternal grandmother went back to school. She completed an undergraduate degree at The College of Mount St. Vincent after working menial jobs in factories and plants. Talk about a miracle and an inspiration! Yes, Elease Huggins Curry was her name, and her DNA runs through my veins; I am proud of her legacy. Our paths have been similar in many ways. I inherited her South Carolinian cooking skills along with my mother's.

I also followed in her footsteps into the world of academia. Granny Elease gave her life to Christ wholeheartedly as a grandmother. She was a faithful member of Mount Hermon Baptist Church in the South Bronx. I visited the church with her a few times in my teens and did a Watch-Night service with her. I felt it was important to attend church with both grandmothers when possible, even though I was closer to my maternal grandmother. Both grandmothers were equally important to me, despite being quite different women. One was northern, Harlem-born, and half West Indian; the other was Southern, from South Carolina, and had come to Harlem as a very young woman. My maternal grandmother raised me and was light, bright, and almost White, while my paternal grandmother was a deep, dark, beautiful chocolate woman. My maternal grandmother only finished eighth grade but traveled to five continents and worked at the renowned Children's Aid Society as an administrative assistant. My grandmother's personality was strong and proud. She co-parented me with my mother, and I lived with her from age thirteen until she was placed in a hospice when I was twenty-four years old. Granny was truly my rock and second mother. In many ways, she influenced me more than she influenced her daughter, my mother.

As I rewind the pages of my life, I can recall memories as far back as the age of two. I vividly recall the lights going out in New York City, which was also the summer of the "Son of Sam." The notorious "Son of Sam" was a killer named David Berkowitz, who went around New York killing random people in the summer of 1977; Berkowitz was a former resident of the neighborhood I grew up in. I remember those events because I looked up one day after nearly three years of happiness, love, joy, and care, and my father was gone.

I do not remember him saying goodbye. My mother says that he wept and took the time to say goodbye to his two-and-a-half-year old daughter, but cognitively, children that age have no concept of finite things such as death, divorce, or separation. My parents were facing issues because my father lost his job after I was born. At the time, New York City was experiencing a fiscal crisis. My father was a Wall Street man who worked for Dreyfus. Being laid off destroyed his marriage, caused him stress, drove him to drink, and turned him into a different person. My mother took on the masculine role; she worked and made money, while my father became the perfect babysitter. My father and I developed a profound connection during this time; I feel like my temperament was more compatible with his than it was with my mother.

When he left, it was a tragic blow. Daddy was a man who cooked, cleaned, played good music, watched children's TV programs with his child, and was a genuinely gifted early childhood educator, despite his lack of formal training. Daddy's disappearance caused me immense trauma. My protector, defender, and playmate were gone. "She" (my mother) put him out of the house a week before the blackout of 1977. The separation was the beginning of a lifelong battle with my mother. I had no idea that my parents were fighting or had problems of any kind. They hid these issues from me. Under the influence of alcohol (mainly beer), my father's personality would change. He would let the devil turn a mellow, cool, logical, intelligent man into a monster. My mother no longer felt safe and did not want her child to see such an example. My father's pride would not allow him to give up his role as a provider, so he lied about paying the rent, leaving my mother in arrears. She had to ask my grandmother to bail them out. His embarrassment made him angry, frustrated, and bitter.

In later years, I asked both of my parents whether it ever occurred to them to pray about their marriage, and both of them said no. I wondered if they had ever prayed together when times were good. They both said, "Unfortunately, Lori, we did not." My father said that they should have and that there was no spiritual application in their marriage. He said, "At that time, I did not know how to introduce any form of spirituality to your mother." My mother agreed, saying, "You're right; we did not invite God into the marriage."

Of course, I asked this question when I was in my late teens and early twenties when I had grown significantly in my knowledge of Christ.

Perhaps if they had incorporated God into their marriage, things would have been very different. Although my father knew more than my mother about the Word of God, they were both un-surrendered, having been a practicing Jehovah's Witness in his teens. Perhaps if he had submitted himself and surrendered totally, our lives would be different, even today. Jehovah's Witness doctrine has its falsehoods, but the people are still very moral. They love their version of the Bible and are faithful missionaries. Then again, I can't see my mother ever being a Jehovah's Witness! Much later, I made them both say the sinner's prayer on various occasions. I truly believe that my mother understood salvation and received it toward the end of her life, Amen. I will discuss my mother's spirituality in a later section of this book because it is a complicated subject.

After my father left the house, my Aunt Cissy, aka Florence Osborne Townsend, quickly replaced him. My mother needed help looking after me between the ages of three and four-and-a-half, so Aunt Cissy became my new caregiver and best friend while my mother was at work. Of course, I still stayed at my maternal grandmother's house across the street every other weekend and sometimes saw her during the week after she finished work. I also spent a lot of time with my great-grandmother in Harlem's Riverton Square, which was and still is a historic and desirable housing complex for middle-income families, where I truly enjoyed spending time. My great-grandmother later became feeble and moved into my grandmother's upgraded, larger apartment in the Bronx. My great-grandmother had been married for about thirty years to her second husband, who was more of a grandfather to my mother than her biological West-Indian grandfather, who had passed away many years before. My step-great-grandfather came from Virginia and was a faithful member of the Abyssinian Baptist Church under the legendary civil-rights activist, Reverend Adam Clayton Powell, Jr. The two of them lived in The Riverton, now known as Riverton Square. Together, they truly enjoyed the historical culture of Black Harlem until my step great-grandfather passed away in 1976. My great-grandmother was steeped in the Episcopalian church, where her whole family had its roots until her husband influenced this shift. My mother was married to her first husband at the Abyssinian Baptist Church. She married my father, her second husband, at the church that she spent her formative years in, St. Luke's Episcopalian Church in Harlem.

My church foundation began with my christening at the Community Protestant Church. The first pastor of CPC was Reverend Ward, a White minister, before Reverend Calvin E. Owens, who became the pastor in late 1976. As far as I know, Owens is still the pastor. I have no personal recollection of Reverend Ward, as I only saw him on an old home movie and heard about him from my mother.

The Community Protestant Church (CPC) was a traditional church, theologically Baptist in nature. Reverend Owens was simply a crossing guard who introduced me to Christ and the gospel at a rudimentary level. I enjoyed what little I can remember of his very foundational teachings. My maternal grandmother and great-grandmother became members of this church. Of course, my grandmother took me with her to the local church because I was dedicated there as a baby, under the previous pastor Reverend Ward. However, Reverend Owens, being African-American changed the congregation's culture and face; CPC became an African American low-key, bourgeoise, family-oriented Baptist church with a great and talented music department that got its "shout on" once or twice a year... at my maternal grandmother's suggestion, I was an active participant in the CPC choir at the age of five and a half. I was directing the choir by middle school, singing solos, ushering, and being a junior deaconess. Phew! That was a lot to take on as a youngster. Of course, I had to give something up, as it was too much. I was getting burnt out and confused about my many roles at church. I had my first shout under that ministry and my first touch of the Holy Spirit, but I wasn't *filled* with the Holy Spirit yet. However, I do believe that it was at CPC that my gifts were stirred (2 Timothy 1:6–7).

By the age of thirteen, I had experienced a great shift, under the influence of my mother's friend Barbara, who had given her life to Christ fully at a Billy Graham crusade. Their mutual friend Dawn also gave her life to

Christ wholeheartedly. Barbara invited Mommy and me to her new wonderful church. I knew there was something very different and special about these Latino and Black people. At my church, people did not bring their Bibles, as these folks did. They did not worship as these folks did, and there was no anointing, as there was at this new church. These folks did not walk out of church and light up cigarettes. Instead, they testified about how they had been delivered from cigarettes, alcohol, and drugs. This church, known as Crossroads Tabernacle, had a reverence for and real connection to God that I had never seen before. This church was a place where it was OK to cry out to God, where heartfelt prayers were said freely, the singing was highly anointed, and the songs were different. This church was a Pentecostal Assembly of God church; the congregants believed in emotional healing, physical healing, signs following, speaking in tongues, and deliverance from former lifestyles that did not please God. Another unusual aspect of this church was that the pastor was a grandmotherly Latina woman who resembled my grandmother. Her name was Aimee Cortese, and her children were all in ministry with her, along with her husband Joe Cortese Sr., the Co-Pastor. After a few visits to the Crossroads Tabernacle, I took my first solo flight to California at the age of thirteen.

I stayed with my cousins in Oakland, California; they were devout Christians, and they showed me what a Spirit-filled, Christian family looked like. I had sinus issues from the air conditioning on the plane to California; by the second day, I was bedridden and struggling to enjoy the visit. "Uncle" Mike laid hands on me, prayed to resolve my sinus issues, and lifted the fever from me. "Uncle" Mike married my "Aunt Merle"; technically, Merle and my mother are same-age 2nd cousins. This laying-on of hands was my first experience of healing through the power of God. I went to church with them as a family. In Oakland, the Shiloh Church was a racially diverse, Spirit-filled church that was totally unlike Community Protestant, which was traditional, with no miracles, signs, or wonders. This visit to Oakland, California, really advanced my transformation that summer. I was being exposed to the Spirit and set free from dead traditionalism.

Scriptural Nugget: Matthew 9:21 NLT
"If I can just touch his robe, I will be healed."

Born Again

That same summer, my mother's friend suggested that I go to the Vacation Bible school for teenagers, sponsored by Crossroads Tabernacle for a week-and-a-half when I was thirteen years old. I went, and the experience changed my entire life because I had a born-again experience, and I met Jesus Christ. My deeper relationship with Him healed my childhood's wounds and transformed me through His love, saving grace, and power. I was one of at least a hundred teenagers in Tannersville, Pennsylvania, at an evening service with Damaris Carbaugh, Pastor Aimee Cortese's daughter. Damaris shared her powerful testimony. After years of trying to have a secular music career, sharing her success stories, and landing a deal with Columbia Records, she surrendered totally and said, "Lord, I just want to sing for your glory." Throughout that week, we teens had sessions with Damaris in which she sang, taught, prayed, and ministered to us.

One night, we all broke under the power of her prayer, and the place was filled with weeping in the Holy Spirit and crying out to God. I asked God to take my life and make it what He wanted it to be. I cried out for authentic salvation and was never the same again. I also climbed Camelback Mountain with the same group of teenagers. We learned that our lives would have mountains, hills, and valley experiences, but with Jesus Christ, we could face every experience, knowing that victory would be ours! I continued to attend the Community Protestant church for a year and a half after that, although it felt very strange to do so. My grandmother belonged to CPC, but when her health began to decline, she stopped attending the church and said that I was free to go where I felt God was leading me. I wanted a deeper walk with God at the house that had administered salvation to me. I thought, "Crossroads Tabernacle, here I come," and there I went.

I can say that Tuesday night prayers at Crossroads taught me how to pray. The prayerful anointing in that house was powerful. There was praise and worship with the lights dimmed, with the praise leaders sitting with the congregation and leading the service with their microphones. The service would include a song, and then a prayer said aloud by members of the congregation, who the Spirit of God moved. Then Pastor Aimee would deliver a Word, with lights still dimmed. Her preaching style was both conversational and anointed. I learned how to pray in that house; as a teenager, I incorporated Tuesday night prayer into my lifestyle. It was there that I encountered the orderly movement of the Holy Spirit, which involved speaking in tongues, interpretation, intercession, and prophetic words, according to (1 Corinthians 14:28). I had not been filled with the Holy Spirit, as described in (Acts 2:4); with the evidence of speaking in tongues.

For this reason, I did not have the power or spiritual maturity to pull down strongholds in my life or the lives of those around me. As a Christian, I was still very carnal, fleshly, moody, and emotional. Although I always felt that I needed more, the church I belonged to did not clearly explain that the evidence of speaking in other tongues was for EVERYONE. I had some great women of God take me under their wings, I confided in them about my life, and they made me aware of the things that were going on in my household that were ungodly that I was scripturally unaware of. I will explore this further in the next few chapters of this book. At that time, I had a Sunday School and a Catholic and Lutheran school background; I constantly studied the Bible between the ages of five and twelve. I continued to study at Crossroads, but not as deeply as I could have. My deep thirst and hunger for the Word of God came about two years later, and I am thankful that it did. Crossroads Tabernacle was predominantly Latino, with members from various other ethnicities. As is typical of the Assemblies of God, they limit the leadership opportunities available to African Americans in their hierarchy. In saying this, I am not implying that Crossroads was deliberately biased; it was a racially inclusive Latino congregation. However, they made it clear that it was a predominantly Latino church, and some people did not always feel included.

When I left the church, I challenged them privately on this matter, and of course, they became angry with me. I believe they have changed and grown, as they now celebrate Black Music Month and have made strong efforts to ensure that all people feel welcome and loved. Overall, the Assemblies of God have some of the most racially diverse congregations in the world. However, its leadership is still predominantly White. Historically, this has been a problem since the Azusa Street revivals of the early 1900s. This racial issue caused the church to split into two Pentecostal sects, the Church of God in Christ for African Americans and the Assemblies of God for White people. I will always say the prayer (Psalm 133:1): "Behold, how good and how pleasant it is for brethren to dwell together in unity!" According to (Galatians 3:28), "There is no longer Jew or Gentile, slave or free, male and female. For you are all one in Christ Jesus."

Growing up in my mother's house was exceedingly difficult but also highly informative. My mother had a hard time after my father left but was never willing to admit this. She deceived herself, me, God, and everyone else, so that she could progress as a single mother. I was the only child born to both my parents. My mother was also an only child. I honestly believe that she did not know how to break certain patterns in her life because she did not understand the cyclical family patterns that plagued her. My mother did not realize that just because her mother or the family did things in a certain way did not make it right, healthy, or the best approach. I was the child who broke the patterns and stepped to the beat of a different drummer. My mother did not always know how to handle me. At my Godmother's suggestion, my mother had my IQ tested for a gifted preschool, and I passed the test. However, my mother did not want to set me up for "too much pressure" and feared that I would become a high-performing, freakish child who was somehow not "normal." I remember this test and the time I spent at that school. I wanted to attend that school, but I never did. At three-and-a-half, my IQ was above average for my age group; when I was tested at ten, the results were similar. Instead, my mother put me in a Catholic elementary school that she felt would invest in me academically and nurture me in a more caring environment with some sort of religious component. By 1981, my Aunt Cissy had moved out to take care of her mother. My great aunt had previously lived with my Godmother, who advised my mother to have me tested. My beautiful Godmother, who married my uncle and was my maternal grandmother's best friend, passed away around that time. Aunt Cissy, therefore, had to step up and leave our house. That was when things got really bad, and I began to suffer intensely. Something had shifted and dramatically changed in my mother. It was devastating to watch.

My mother tried to resolve the pain of her second marriage's failure through men, alcohol, and an ever-increasing nicotine habit that I hated my whole life. She went into denial and presented a perfect front to the world, acting as if everything was fine and ignoring God, who could have saved her My grandmother, an early resident of the then mainly White Co-op City, lived up the street from my mother. By the time I was three, I regularly spent weekends at her house. In 1979, when I was four-and-a-half, there was a new gentleman in my mother's life (she had divorced my father earlier that year) My father joined the Corrections Academy in 1979 and completed training to work at the Downstate Correctional Facility, a new correctional facility in Fishkill, New York. He took this job hoping that he could reunite with his family and win back his wife and child, but this dream was never actualized.

God is truly amazing because, even when we believe that we know what's best, God has a much better plan. About two-and-a-half years later, the man my mother was involved with tragically died of cancer. This loss shook my mother and rocked her to her core, causing her to go into therapy. My mother's behavior toward me began to change for the worse, and she became hostile. She began to abuse me verbally, saying demeaning things that eroded my self-confidence. It would have been better if she had cursed me out or used profanity. You don't have to use profane words to be abusive, and my mother had an extensive vocabulary. Sometimes, she would tell me that I was pretty, beautiful, sensitive, and intelligent. She often praised me and told me that I was a wonderful child with unlimited possibilities. However, the very next day, she might say that I'd be lucky to be "half the woman" she was. These words were spoken by a woman who was broken during childhood. The same things had probably been said to her. She may not have understood the kind of cyclical damage that she was causing and passing down.

All this hurt and pain was inflicted by someone I was supposed to trust. My mother was not the sweet woman who loved me when I was a small child, speaking to me kindly but firmly. My mother's after-hours drinking began to increase at a rate that I was uncomfortable with as a child. I saw her adopt very self-destructive patterns, or perhaps these patterns were there but did not manifest on a larger scale until pain reared its ugly head. Thankfully, my mother was able to find professional assistance. However, she needed so much more; in truth, she needed the Lord Jesus Christ in her life.

After the death of a boyfriend whom she felt deeply connected to, she had relationships with a series of men. I woke up seeing some of these men in my house. On many occasions, I was shipped across the street to my grandmother's house when my mother went out or entertained "company." I knew in my soul that I did not want to be like her. Once I acquired the saving knowledge of who Jesus was and began to attend a Bible-believing, Spirit-filled church, my eyes were opened. Seasoned people in God counseled me to leave my household. Several people told me that there were occult spirits and spiritual witchcraft in my mother's household, and these energies felt normal to me before I was made aware of what they were. I will never forget two women, both named Linda, who gave me wise counsel. They told me that my mother was into witchcraft and that her home was spiritually unsafe. My same feelings were confirmed several times by people who were all saved and Spirit-filled. Although they did not know each other, they said that I needed to get out. In 1989, my mother met a man. Three months later, she moved this man into the apartment that she and my father had set up. Four months later, she married him, only knowing that he had a degree and a well-paid job and appeared to be a well-spoken, intelligent person. What bothered me most was how quickly my mother embraced this relationship. She behaved, almost like a woman in her twenties. It bothered me that this man had recently left a deep relationship with a girlfriend, moved in with his mother, and then, very quickly, moved in with my mother. He had no children of his own, no real experience with children other than his nieces and nephews and had never wanted children. What my mother chose to overlook was that he was addicted to cocaine and also an alcoholic. Although his face was scarred from a previous alcohol-induced car accident, my mother did not want to acknowledge this. She may not have known until afterward that his own drunk driving caused the accident. I thought this whole scenario was strange; it felt wrong to me. At this point, my mother and I had been living together as mother and daughter for twelve years. Our mother-and-daughter fights suddenly became this man's business. Feeling that he had to protect my mother from me, he began to physically abuse me, not beating me black and blue but roughing me up in a way that was totally inappropriate for a man who had just met me and was not even married to my mother yet. She never intervened, never stopped the abuse, and never found it odd or strange. Instead, she continued her relationship with him. She even asked me to leave my own house and go to my grandmother's place one night before he moved in so that the two of them could be together. My mother's position set the tone, allowing this man to disrespect me going forward. He was clearly envious of the bond I had with my mother, which he had never had with his own mother.

When establishing a new family, one must carefully vet one's new spouse, especially when there is a child from a prior marriage. I had to learn to forgive my mother for this betrayal. She sold me out for the love of a man who did not even love himself or God. I had to forgive her for being desperate enough to allow herself to be deceived by her own flesh. I swore that I would never allow this to happen to my child. During years of voluntary therapy throughout my teens, I worked through the hows and the whys. Through the deliverance I sought, I broke dysfunctional patterns and became the child that my parents conceived and gave birth to, with none of their self-destructive patterns. With the help of God almighty, I was able to overcome the negative attributes I could have absorbed, overthrowing the enemy's early plans. As time went on, my grandmother's health slowly declined, having been diagnosed with her first brain tumor in 1987. As my great-grandmother, who lived with my grandmother in Co-op City, declined and approached her transition in 1986, I believe that my grandmother's health also took a turn for the worse. Her brain tumor situation affected her speech post-operatively. My grandmother was a very prideful woman, and she withdrew socially as the years passed, and her health gradually declined over the next ten years. My grandmother's care protected me from my mother's dysfunctional household and created a happier environment. I had both spiritual freedom and a lack of supervision; these forced me to grow up and become more independent. My mother parented me remotely. If I needed to, I could see her once or twice a week by going across the street. However, I preferred our phone conversations. My father lived seventy miles away in upstate New York. He wasn't a consistent presence during my childhood because he had substance abuse issues and emotional pain following his divorce from my mother. By the time I was fifteen, my mother had a new man in her life, and my father miraculously pulled things together. I talked to my father every day, apart from the one time when I chose not to speak to him for a month or so. That was intentional and not because he couldn't reach me. Otherwise, my father and I saw each other every couple of months and talked every day until his passing in 2015.

My father was truly my friend. We had an extraordinary bond that developed when I was little. In 1977 my mother provided for our household, while my father was a stay-at-home dad, creatively and wonderfully taking care of his pre-school daughter, who was talking, walking, singing, and dancing well beyond her years. I loved the time I spent with my father that year. He was very nurturing. When he needed an adult diversion, we took the train to Harlem's Riverton Square to visit and spend the afternoon with my great-grandmother, which I always enjoyed. The tensions between my parents seemed to escalate when my father lost his job with Dreyfus. He lied to my mother about paying the rent because he was proud and afraid of his mother-in-law, who lived across the street. As a result, he owed back rent, which caused an ugly situation. According to my mother, these financial worries caused my father to become depressed. He began drinking heavily, backed my mother into a corner, made a fist, and physically threatened her. This incident marked the end of their relationship. My mother no longer felt safe with her husband and did not want her daughter to grow up in such an environment. I have absolutely no recollection of them ever fighting or even arguing, as they were intelligent enough to keep me out of their crazy drama. I was not raised in a household filled with alcoholism or domestic violence. I can honestly say that I never saw my father "falling down" drunk, as he was careful to protect me from that image. Although I heard him intoxicated over the phone a couple of times, I only witnessed him intoxicated once, at the age of thirty-two, before leaving New York in 2007. On that occasion alone, I saw the Jekyll-and-Hyde personality change that my mother described. Otherwise, I commend my father for protecting me as well as he could from his issues. Thank God I never saw the wife-batterer, the violent man who remembered nothing, or the out-of-control monster who was always angry. I heard this behavior over the phone, but I never saw it in person.

Over the years, I begged him to get help. My Middle School Guidance Counselor asked me a series of questions and deduced that my father was a functioning alcoholic. He was too prideful—and considered himself too intelligent and under control—to admit that he had a problem. His intellectually arrogant ego would not allow him to look at the issue honestly and get help. I tried to evangelize and to pray with and for him. I begged God for him, but he couldn't fully surrender. Although I know he loved God, his will was too weak. I prayed the sinner's prayer with him a few times, bought him Bibles, and wrote long letters trying to save him, but his will and ego made that impossible. I believe that my father genuinely loved God and sought him during his teenage years, as he traveled door-to-door with the Jehovah's Witnesses. He also had a spiritual church mother named "Mother Johnson," who took him to fellowship with her at a Holiness-Pentecostal Seventh Day Adventist church. Although this was good for my father, his marriage to his first wife (not my mother) did not enhance his spiritual quest. His first wife was Catholic, and he studied the catechism in order to marry her. This proves that his own spiritual convictions were not solid; I believe that he could have done well serving in ministry with proper guidance in some capacity.

By the age of fifteen, I had moved into my grandmother's house as a brokenhearted teen, taking care of my grandmother, who was also taking care of me. My mother turned my room into an office for her new husband, whom I had only known for three months. First, she moved him into the house as her live-in lover. Then she told me to stay at my grandmother's house so that she and her husband could have private time. This treatment crushed me. I also wondered what kind of man would move out of his ex-girlfriend's house, into his mother's house, and then into my mother's house, where her ex-husband (my father) used to live? Who does that and feels good about himself? I knew that these adults were completely out of their minds. My mother allowed a man to live in our home, physically put his hands on me, and rough me up physically. She allowed me to be abused and driven out of my own home by a total stranger, whom she subsequently discovered was an addict with a suit, tie, good job, and degree. I knew that there was something wrong with him, but lust, desperation, and fear of the saving knowledge of Jesus Christ will make a person do things that oppose logic, maturity, and common sense. The reality of my situation was that I was not safe. Although my biological father was caught up in his world, this situation made him a consistent figure in my life. My father was more willing to listen than ever before, and he provided more emotional support, although he felt it was better for me to stay at my grandmother's house, where it was safe.

I grew closer to the Lord throughout this time and happier with myself, as I no longer had to live in fear, depression, and sorrow. I still had to fight depression, but the joy of the Lord was my strength. Before I moved out of my mother's house, I did not have the emotional strength to stay in school. I also thought that I was too intelligent to be with my peers. My goal was to work in a recording studio, write songs, make music, and live the life of some sort of artist. I preferred to stay home, jam, write, cook, and do more mature, intellectual "grown-up" things. I thought my peers were childish. When I was in the 11th grade, I opted to take my GED due to my inability to pass math. My choosing to leave high school was difficult for my family to process. They were very disappointed by this.

All the while, I was singing in the choir and faithfully attending Bible study and Tuesday night prayers. I learned to love being in the house of the Lord because it strengthened me. I carried my life of prayer, incorporating the Word of God into my daily life, as well as I could. I had no blueprint or idea of how a saved household should look; my older maternal cousins in Oakland were the only saved household I knew. So, immediately before I gave my heart to Christ, I had nothing to go on. I had to navigate my spirituality on my own. Although my parents were confessing believers who knew what was right, they simply did not have the power or internal conviction for attempting to apply any spiritual principles until much later. In 1993, at the age of eighteen, I received the results of my GED exam; I had passed at the top of my alternative high-school class with the highest score. Although I was the valedictorian, I did not show up for graduation. I just wanted to go to college. Before I turned eighteen, I continued to attend church faithfully. Increasingly, however, the Assemblies of God church that I loved so much began to seem a bit clannish, which was only natural, given that the leadership was Latino, as were most of the congregants. Unfortunately, African American people at this church were rarely selected for solos in the choir. When confronted on this point, the church leaders became offended.

I had to move on to grow. I found a church that was closer to home in Mount Vernon because I did not want to return to the childhood church my grandmother and great-grandmother had attended. Once I had experienced the church that ushered in my true salvation, I no longer wanted to return to the church I was raised in, as I saw no life in it. To backtrack, in 1983, my father took up residency with his common-law wife, whom he legally married toward the end of his life. He became a stepfather figure to his new wife's daughter. My father's third wife became his longest relationship and union. The other two marriages, including his marriage to my mom, were not comparable in length or duration. My father found a community of enablers in which he could feel comfortable being who he "thought" he was, namely, a functioning alcoholic who would not be questioned, challenged, or told to get help. It was normal in his community to drink beer heavily, as long as you could go to work and pay your bills. In his community, you were OK. By the time I was seventeen, I had linked up with a group of teenagers in the neighborhood who also had family and educational challenges. My best friend was moving away to be with her long-lost father, whom she had never met in her life. Losing the girl who had been my best friend since I was twelve was traumatic. We had been through everything together, and I felt I had no support after she left. She was my singing partner and my partner in pain and heartache. We found refuge in each other because we had an emotional understanding. Although she came from a White Jewish background, she was as soulful as any Black girl. Unlike me, Celeste was from the Marble Hill projects and had experienced the South West Bronx.

It gave her a toughness I didn't possess. She knew how to be intimidating when I had not learned that yet. I learned it not long after.

Celeste and I had done everything together, putting up with each other's moods and profound, sweeping adolescent changes. When she left, it reopened some unresolved abandonment issues left over from childhood. Losing my Godmother at six was traumatic because she and my father both encouraged my love of music and singing. Losing my uncle (my Godmother's husband) a few years earlier had also been traumatic. Then I experienced my parents' separation and my Aunt Cissy's loss, who lived with me intermittently to help my mother cope after my parents split. My great-grandmother left us when I was eleven, and I was blessed to have her that long. Back-to-back losses and family disappearances made my mother feel, in her own words, "like a Holocaust victim." My early childhood was plagued with loss, disappointment, and a mother who tried to hold things together outwardly while inwardly falling apart.

I was seventeen years old and hanging with a new fast crowd, which was the antithesis of everything I was raised to be and knew. It was a rebellious crew of teens; one girl I ran with for about a year was fast and believed that her feminine power was between her legs. This young girl was broken-hearted, did not live with her mom, and was raised by her father. Spending time with her, I began to explore my sexuality. I became promiscuous, having had my heart broken after my first sexual experience at seventeen. The friend I met in the street when my mother asked me to leave became my protector. I adopted him as an older brother figure. He never flirted with me when I first met him. However, when I was almost eighteen, he did. He was nine years older than me, and when he was released from jail, he became my lover. Young girls in urban areas fall victim to this behavior every day if they have selfish parents who also had self-centered parents and do not know how to break negative familial patterns. Of course, my father did not approve of this on-and-off relationship with a much older man who had previously been in jail, but believe it or not, my dad liked him. They had many phone conversations but never actually met. I trusted my father as a good judge of character, and he was much more down-to-earth than my mother.

Although my father was highly intelligent and well-spoken, with an extensive vocabulary, he had a street edge and could relate to people from all walks of life better than my super-intelligent yet bourgeois mother. Although my parents had very different upbringings and experiences that shaped them in similar ways, their lives had many contrasting factors.

In 1993, I officially removed myself from this gentleman because some of his negative characteristics did not change. He was a Muslim who believed in Jesus but did not convert. He was a very well-meaning and caring person, but he wasn't for me because I had grown and changed. I didn't want to be around him any longer because we were better off as friends. Over the years, I have tried to stay in touch because I was thankful for the support he provided during a rough season of my life. In life, we outgrow those people who can't even help themselves. Today, I would not choose half the people I made friends with back then. However, I was trying to figure out life on my own. Although my mother talked to me about life and tried her best to be involved, even from across the street, I was still dealing with the gravity of my grandmother's illness, and she was slowly losing her neurological and physical faculties. Even after two brain-tumor operations, my maternal grandmother came in a thunderstorm to pick me up from school because I needed an adult to take me home. As I stood outside, waiting for her, the wind and rain were beating up her umbrella. She was walking with a struggle, and I became emotional as I watched her inch toward the school to get me, her granddaughter.

I was loved—in fact, I was adored. Despite how messed up my main caretakers and their issues may have been, I know that I was loved. Unfortunately, my grandmother could not supervise me as a teenager as she had done when I was younger because of her condition, but she was still attentive and aware. I could not pull the wool over my grandmother's eyes. Even in her most debilitated state, she was a warrior like her mother Helen, her mother's mother Emma, and her mother Louisa, before her. Louisa was a rebellious warrior slave in Virginia. When you know where you come from, you tend to have a better idea of where you're going and what you're made of.

Living with my grandmother was like having my own place. I was my own little woman, creating my own rules within limits. Yes, I snuck boys in, experimented with weed, and skipped school, but my grandmother intervened because she was concerned. She also got my mother involved, from her house across the street, of course. While all of this was going on, I was still attending church with the assistance of good and wise, Spirit-Filled Christians. I was held accountable and felt convicted of taking God's grace for granted. I knew the word but had not yet committed to deep, intense study. I had a dedicated prayer life but was not yet Spirit-Filled. For this reason, I was a very carnal baby Christian who was hurting. I was not yet discipled in godliness or holiness. I was getting there, slowly but surely. A friend of mine from church, who was relatively new in Christ herself but older than me by about nine years, decided to leave the church we were attending for a multicultural church that seemed non-traditional but offered to provide intense Bible study under the guise of "discipleship." I tagged along with my sister-friend, although I was cautious and apprehensive because these folks seemed a little too friendly and a little too aggressive about wanting to meet me. One young lady was operating in the spirit of witchcraft, which I will discuss later in the book. When I refer to witchcraft here, I am not referring to Obeah, Voodoo, Hoodoo, Santeria, or Wicca; instead, I am referring to a spirit of control. I don't even remember this lady's name, but I remember that she was passionate about the Bible; these folks were a part of the international Churches of Christ (ICOC), a body of co-operating,[5] religiously conservative, and racially integrated[4] Christian congregations. Beginning with thirty members, they grew to 37,000 members within the first twelve years. Currently, they have more than 110,000 members.[6] They broke from the mainline Churches of Christ in 1993, organizing the ICOC. According to the ICOC the whole Bible is the inspired word of God and the people are saved by the grace of God when they place their faith in and trust and become disciples of **Jesus Christ**, repent, and are baptized.

[7]This family of churches is spread across some 155 nations.[4] The churches consider themselves non-denominational,[4] and they are structured in a way that avoids two extremes: "overly centralized authority," on the one hand, anddescribed as "[a] fast-growing Christian organization, known for

aggressive proselytizing to [U.S.] college students" and also as "one of the most controversial religious groups on campus."[10] The largest congregation, the Los Angeles Church of Christ, had over 6000 members.[3] The largest church service was held in 2012 at the AT&T Center in San Antonio, Texas, during a World Discipleship Summit with 17,800 attendees.[11][12] (Source Wikipedia). The most disturbing thing about this group was this: if you wanted to study the Bible with them, they treated you as if you were not a Christian, even if you were already saved and belonged to another church. The ICOC did not think anyone was Christian outside their organization. If you thought you were already a Christian, you had to "unlearn" everything you were ever taught because you could not be a Christian outside the ICOC unless you were made into a disciple by one of their rank-and-file disciple leaders. They were judgmental, condemning, and crossed significant boundaries with those they were "discipling" by looking for sin and forcing themselves into people's lives. The ICOC would call people late at night, demanding that they disclose intimate details of their lives to a discipler, even if they had not built any rapport. The ICOC had wonderful dinner parties with great food called "*Bible Talks*" at the apartments of people who lived in the city. If you were a new face, everyone would seem very interested in "getting to know you." My church warned me about this group, and I quickly realized that I was not comfortable with them. Although they held extravagant functions, the Bible-study group made me extremely depressed. I felt that they were attempting to erode my self-esteem and make me question everything I knew. Something felt wrong: the legalism, rules, and measuring up in God's sight were all particularly important, while grace, mercy, and love were in short supply. Even when they pretended to love and care about you, the underlying message was that God was out to get you and that you would never measure up. Such emotions are not of God—they are of Satan. Conviction can certainly be the Holy Spirit's work, but condemnation cannot (Romans 8:1–2).

After experiencing this group, I recognized that it was not of God. The elders in my church confirmed this when I discussed it with them. I no longer fellowshipped (visited) with the ICOC. Thank God I was not foolish enough to join. The Holy Spirit gave me enough discernment to understand what real Christian fellowship felt like. Everything that I felt was strange, and I broke off my relationship with the sister, who became deeply involved with this organization. About four or five years later, the ICOC was featured in the TV news, which dedicated a whole segment to exposing this "cult" or Christian church with controlling, cult-like practices, which it claimed were psychologically and socially damaging. This news report confirmed what I already knew. I was so glad I had not been caught up with this group, as my friend had. After breaking off ties with her, I later reached out to this sister to ask what she thought of her church's media exposure. She said the group had changed and repented of their aggressive and condemning discipleship tactics. She chose to remain and may still be a part of this group today. Others have told me that the group has toned down its tactics, but I've met people from states as far away as California who were damaged by this group and had a very legalistic view of God because this was their first introduction to who God is. Discernment is critical when it comes to recognizing cults. Cults can manifest even in so-called Christian churches. An organization can be Bible-based, founded on Scripture, and still have cultish behavior and recruitment tactics. Because of my background and experiences, God has given me a burden involving cults and spiritually deviant organizations, countering Christ in their theology.

One prominent characteristic of a cult is ostracizing anyone whose beliefs differ. Such people can be cut off, dismissed, "marked," and identified as dissenters within the group. Dynamics like this can be psychologically damaging to any "dissenter" or group member who wants to be free of the destructive group. Leaving destructive groups and organizations can be draining; leaving can be just as traumatic as belonging to the group. I will talk more about cults, both Christian and non-Christian, in later chapters. However, discernment is critical, and we must pray to be as wise as serpents and as harmless as doves, as Jesus said (Matthew 10:6). As a result of my previous encounters with certain groups, I have truly developed a sensitivity to dangerous groups. Red flags go up immediately when I sense manipulation or control in an organization's leadership style or methods. Crossroads was my safe haven until I no longer felt welcome because I brought certain things to the leadership's attention. In 1992, I tuned into a radio station at the end of the New York City dial, which broadcasted live from a church in Mount Vernon, New York. I renewed my search for the Holy Spirit. I considered returning to the African American church after being in a Latino Assemblies of God church that was diverse but not sufficiently inclusive.

Scriptural Nugget: 2 Corinthians 6:17 NLT

"Therefore, come out from among unbelievers, and separate yourselves from them, says the LORD. Don't touch their filthy things, and I will welcome you."

The Regeneration

After listening to the radio and hearing Pastor C.N. Edwers preach, I felt it was time to return to my roots, but with people who seemed more devoted and Spirit-filled than the African American congregation of my childhood. Edwers was in his mid-twenties with a great wife and very young children. He was highly educated and had an older person's wisdom, seeming more like forty-five than twenty-six years old. I used to take a cab to his church at a very low price, instead of taking a bus and the train. The cab ride took only twelve minutes and was much easier than waiting for buses and trains to commute to a place that was forty minutes away. Although it became a bit costly for an eighteen-year-old to take cabs back and forth, I persevered. I grew a lot in the Unified Freewill Baptist Church and learned that it was a full gospel Baptist church, where people believed in the gifts of the Spirit, as Pentecostals do while following Baptist theology. At this point in my life, I was leaning more toward Pentecostalism. I saw the devotion that people displayed in church but did not see much change in their personal lives.

Perhaps I was judgmental in this assessment. However, I saw power on display in the church, but only limited power present in people's lives. The friendships I made there were special, as great spiritual mothers on the mother board truly loved congregants into life. There was much praise, breakthroughs truly occurred, and it was a house of love. In no way was it a cold church. Bishop Edwers (then simply Pastor Edwers) was very personable and hands-on. His assistant pastor often took me to her house, where we had real conversations about life and the reality and woes of ministry. Even my mother liked her, although many people in the church wished that my mother would support me in the church setting. She rarely did because she could not relate to the places that grew me spiritually.

The church reared me and raised me. This was my reality, and I am so thankful for every person who prayed me through and ministered to me in my youth. In my teens, I studied various teachings that were circulating in New York. Everyone adopted Muslim names because of the 5% doctrine and Islamic trends in Hip Hop; culturally aware New York teens in the African American community tended to want "knowledge of self." Yes, I even studied the Tarikhe Tarsile version of the Quran. Between Farrakhan on the radio on Sunday mornings and Dr. York, aka Imam Issa's Ansar Allah and Nubian Islamic Hebrew books circulating around the city, most young people were influenced by Islam unless they had "super religious" parents who forbade them from exploring anything but Christianity. Most of the information was Bible-based and very positive, promoting good morals and values. Many of us felt that these movements gave us more moral discipline than we could find in our churches.

When we saw the Ansar Allah sisters wearing their White garb or "a Niqab" as they used to say, we wanted to wear the same thing and smell like Frankincense oil. There was certain regal righteousness about it. The half-naked girls in Hip Hop did not come from the north. Instead, such misogynistic behavior seemed to begin with Luther Campbell and "*2 Live Crew*" in Miami. Later, this same presentation of women also appeared in the West Coast Hip Hop scene. In these two regions, Islam was less prevalent than in New York City, where it had a moral impact on popular music. Being curious, I loved the fact that this alternative information was available. It gave me a sense of cultural pride. However, it could also be dangerous. People who were not seasoned in God could be drawn away from Christ by other doctrines. Many people have testified that Dr. York made young people study and dissect the Bible, unlike the local preacher, who did not make young people want to dig deep or seek the truth of the Word of God.

I know this sounds strange, but it took a Muslim cult leader to make young New Yorkers in the 1990s pull apart the Scriptures and become well versed in them. So, these diverse groups were beneficial. By providing study guides and challenging us to determine the truth of God's Word, they made us open up the Word of God even further. Under the direction of Bishop Edwers, I was allowed to speak, testify, and share at the podium at a youth conference at a church in Brooklyn. It was the first time I was given the opportunity to speak a word. As I did not know what to say, I spoke what the Lord had given to me. I discussed, "He that hath an ear let him hear what the Spirit says unto the church" from Revelations, Chapter 2. It was certainly not my best speech or "sermonette." However, Bishop Edwers was attempting to groom me for ministry, although I did not realize it at the time. He was mentoring me, and I felt honored and humbled by the opportunity. He was stirred by the anointing displayed during my Sunday church-choir solos and invited me to the youth conference. He saw something that I did not yet see in myself. From my perspective, I was just singing a song, but the congregation caught fire with the Holy Spirit. Perhaps I did not take it seriously enough at the time. I did not want to become big-headed or to see myself as a new phenomenon in his ministry. To be honest, I feared the anointing of God on my life. I was just a nineteen-year-old who was trying to find my way in the Lord and to walk more deeply with Him than I had the day before. I still felt that I was missing something.

Just one year earlier, I had been out in the world after being hurt in church, confused by the New York City Church of Christ, aka ICOC. I felt that if I held on to Jesus while throwing myself into the world to discover what I was really "saved" from, I would develop new insights and gain a deeper testimony. I tried to think of anything that I was bold enough and bad enough to do in 1992–1993. I fornicated and lost my virginity at seventeen, having made out with boys since my pre-teen years. I go-go danced three times for the money to go to Six Flags while reading the Bible in the back of the club before go-go dancing. In fact, I was out of my mind. I watched porno flicks when I could and tried weed, cigarettes, and alcohol, but I could not get addicted to ANYTHING . I didn't like what I was trying to do or who I was trying to be. Although I tried clubbing a few times and went out dancing all night long, I just couldn't get into that lifestyle. None of it lasted, satisfied me, or turned me on. It was just too late. I had already tasted and seen that the Lord was and is good. I missed God and His presence. I felt like I was going to get myself killed. At the time, my boyfriend was "thuggin," and I was trying to be "thugged out," even though that was NOT who I was raised to be. Therefore, I cut my ties with these friends and, by the time I began studying under Bishop Edwers, I was seeking a stronger connection with the Holy Spirit. I needed more and began to read my great Aunt's Bible. Although she had been gone for about five years, she had been an Episcopalian lady who loved the Lord and had a very deep prayer life. As I opened this Bible, which was given my grandmother when her aunt passed, it still had her scent on it, a sort of "old people" scent, if that makes any sense. This Bible was seriously anointed. I had read the Bible all my life, but this was a Thompson Chain Study Bible. I had never experienced anything like it. This Bible made all of the pieces of my life fit together, like no other Bible I had ever read before. For some reason, I could NOT put this Bible down; I was addicted to the Word of God. My soul burned within me every time I opened this Bible (Luke 24:32). Some might say, "well, Lori, you took all of these detours—what was going on with you?" I would say, "He knows the way that I take" (Job 23:10).

Many of God's main leaders stumbled on their journeys. Even when they went astray, they never stopped seeking God. As I began to read more of the Scripture, the Lord guided me toward studying more about the power of the Holy Spirit. Friendship Church had many manifestations of the Holy Spirit. I had already experienced shouting, crying, praising, and worshipping, both privately and within congregations, in my young life. However, I wanted to know more about speaking in tongues, as this was the evidence of the Holy Spirit; I wanted to know whether this was real, according to (Acts 2:4). Therefore, I continued to pray and seek God's Holy Spirit, as evidenced by speaking in other tongues. I studied every Scripture on the indwelling of the Holy Spirit. However, as soon as I opened my mouth and tried to speak, it felt awkward and weird. I began to watch an old man preaching on UHF TV in New York. Does anyone remember UHF channels, those local stations that you could get even without cable? They were usually on the dial between Channels 14 and 83. I loved this spunky old man who preached and talked about being Pentecostal. His congregation would ecstatically go in all the way when he preached. I discovered that this pastor was the late great Bishop William Lee Bonner at the Greater Refuge Temple (GRT) of Harlem, New York. At this time, I was a singer on New York City's Kiss Inspirations Choir, which was a radio choir formed by personnel from New York City's now-defunct radio station, Kiss FM. Many on this choir were of the Apostolic faith, and I asked certain people on the choir if they knew who this man "Bonner" was, and they advised me to visit and pursue the infilling of the Holy Spirit with the evidence of speaking in other tongues. I told myself that I would go to see him soon because his sermons ignited something in me. I thought that Bonner was a fearless preacher who wasn't afraid of anything.

As he often said, this was because he knew that he served an invincible God. I also discovered that Bonner had an AM radio show on Saturday evenings, and I began to listen to his teachings at night before bed. I could hear the congregation going insane on these tapes, as his messages were very powerful. Sometimes I would fall asleep during the broadcast because his show was on between 10 and 11 pm, if my memory serves me right. After studying about the Holy Spirit for some time, I fell asleep one night to Bishop Bonner preaching about the Holy Ghost. I remember drifting off; at the climactic close of his sermon, I heard myself speaking in tongues in my sleep. I could feel the bed shaking, and when I opened my eyes, I was speaking in other tongues as the spirit of God gave the utterance.

A few months later, in early 1994, I returned to the same building as my mother and her husband, after three-and-a-half years of living across the street in a beautiful apartment with memories of people who passed on. This residence included my great-grandmother and other visitors. Given my grandmother's failing health, my mother finally stepped up and acquired an apartment for my grandmother and me on the same floor that she lived on. One of the neighbors had passed away, and the apartment became available. I felt sick, both emotionally and physically, at having to go back to that particular floor, building, and residence. It felt like I was re-victimized and re-traumatized. I lost 15 pounds and looked like I had a disease or was taking drugs. My weight dropped to 119 pounds, and I felt like I was dying spiritually, physically, and emotionally. The pain, fear, and resentment were too much for me to bear. However, I managed to move and sought spiritual help. I began pressing closer into my God again. My grandmother had developed a third brain tumor and did not respond to treatment but hung on to life. By this time, I had completed cosmetology school and passed the state board exam to become a licensed cosmetologist; my mother served as my live head of hair participant.

Scriptural Nugget: Acts 1:8 (NLT)
"But you will receive power when the Holy Spirit comes upon you. And you will be my witnesses, telling people about me everywhere-in Jerusalem, throughout Judea, in Samaria, and to the ends of the earth."

The Greatest Refuge

I realized that I had to go to Harlem to visit The Greater Refuge Temple. First, I made an appointment to "tarry" for the Holy ghost with the GRT, and one of the "mothers" met me before the Tarrying service in the "upper room," as they called it. A mother prayed with me a few times; she assessed that I had "stammering tongues" and needed to break through further. I later learned from other seasoned saints that, like any language, and may not flow freely at first. The more I prayed and spoke, the more my prayer language developed. With it came the gifts of healing and prophecy; deliverance was, and probably still is, in my hands. Many of these things frightened me when they began to manifest. I started to attend the GRT frequently, although some important doctrinal issues were very different from what I had been taught. The Church of Our Lord Jesus Christ (COOLJC) taught congregants that the initial formula for salvation was based upon Acts 2:38: "Repent and be baptized every one of you in the name of the Lord Jesus Christ for the remission of sins and you shall receive the gift of the Holy Ghost."

According to their interpretation of (Romans 8:9), those who did not have the Holy Spirit were not God's children. According to COOLJC, if you did not speak in tongues, you were not saved. Also, if you did not go down in the water in the name of the Lord Jesus Christ, your baptism was invalid, jeopardizing your salvation. According to the doctrine of COOLJC, the Great Commission instructions that Jesus gave to his disciples in (Matthew 28:19) were a mystery. The instructions were, "Go into all the world and make disciples, baptizing them in the name of the Father and of the Son and the Holy Ghost." COOLJC argued that this was a mystery that needed to be revealed because the Trinity was a Catholic invention; the word "Trinity" does not appear in the Bible. At COOLJC, the Father God was the Lord, the name of the Son was Jesus, and the Holy Spirit was the Christ. They baptized in the name of the Lord Jesus Christ and considered other forms of baptism invalid. This idea never sat right with me, although it was very logical. However, this theological theory did not address the original languages or the meaning of the name Jesus, derived from the Greek Iyesous, instead of the original Hebrew, which was Yeshua (His name) Ha Mashiach (His title) According to Bonner, those who had a Trinitarian baptism were baptized in the title and not the name; no one could be "saved" unless they were baptized in Jesus' name and spoke in tongues. In (John 3:5), Jesus says, "you must be born of the water and the Spirit." COOLJC interpreted this "water" as baptism, even though it could simply refer to a person being born first from his mother's womb and then into the Spirit, experiencing a "new birth." Many young people and I at that time were beginning to question leadership. Young people requested a meeting with the leadership of the GRT in 1996 to discuss the foundation of the doctrine.

Although I did not attend, I still had my say. I loved the GRT, and I always will. I have seen them take heed and loosen up a bit about earrings, nail polish, and quite a few other things in recent years. Men could not wear full beards; this now seems to be very much allowed, judging from recent COOLJC conferences and videos. Greater Refuge and COOLJC are now allowing other Spirit-filled preachers who do not belong to their organization to preach at their conferences. I am glad to see this. I learned so much in the GRT, and I loved the Apostolic Holiness teachings. I lived the Christian life to the best of my abilities and did not come to church to play games. This Christian walk was a serious subject for me. Although I was still imperfect, I put in the time to feast on the word and began to see significant changes in my life. At Greater Refuge, I went to the altar to pray as needed when Bishop Bonner was there, and I learned so much from the caring, seasoned, and truly saved women in GRT. I used to sit in the meditation room with a mother I loved dearly and prayed quietly until the Spirit moved. I then entered into His presence, and God broke my chains. There was so much deliverance in the Temple. GRT was not just a worshipping or Pentecostal experience; sound biblical doctrine was always delivered from the pulpit. At that time, Bishops James I. Clark Jr. and Charles Wright (then Elder Wright) were the two associate pastors. Bishop Bonner showed up once a month and stayed for a few days before bouncing to another one of his U.S. churches. So, when Bishop Bonner came, we were always thrilled to see him. People would say, "Poppa's coming home," since the GRT was the headquarters of COOLJC. One Sunday, when Apostle Bonner walked down the aisle to shake every member's hand, he made sure that he touched all 2,000 people. When he came to me, I just wept with a smile and shook his hand. I prayed that God would enable me to have the same spiritual vitality and impact as Bonner. I met people who were truly striving to live this journey of holiness and total devotion to Christ Jesus. I can truly say that, after receiving the baptism in the Holy Spirit, as evidenced by my speaking in other tongues, I have never gone back to reckless or self-destructive patterns in my life. I will not pretend that I have never committed a sin or messed up, but I never again adopted a lifestyle that would not please God. I loved GRT and the wonderful people I met there, who helped me grow and develop. Many good women poured into me. Even some great men of God took the time to explain the ins and outs of ministry and life in Christ. The time that I spent achieving deliverance from childhood and teenage woes was well worth it. There were many tears, lots of time spent lying on the floor, and lots of fasting, prayer, and all-night prayers with young people at the church. I fought hard for my healing and deliverance and got it. Even my therapist saw the difference in me and said that we no longer needed to see each other in sessions. I later joined the Daughters of Jerusalem, a group designed for young women who were thinking about becoming missionaries in the future. We wanted to serve in similar capacities but needed training, grooming, and preparation for greater things while still doing the work of young missionaries. I believe the roles progressed from Daughter of Jerusalem to Junior Missionary, Missionary, and Senior Missionary. Similarly, young men started as Junior Deacons before moving into the Ministry and becoming Elders if God called them into that role.

The Daughters of Jerusalem were responsible for altar work, intercessory prayer, baptism preparations (in some cases, getting in the water with some of the saints to be baptized), and assisting the Pastors with this duty. The Daughters tarried with new souls for the Holy Spirit, sometimes for hours, as well as doing outreach and evangelism, visiting the sick and people who were shut in, making nursing-home visits, and being available to all of the saints as needed for church prayers, but with a focus on women. I enjoyed the Daughters of Jerusalem, who seemed "super deep" to me at the time. I devoted myself to holiness; I knew there was so much religiosity in the role because of the doctrine of the COOLJC. It was forbidden to listen to secular music, go to movies, wear makeup and earrings, or date people from other churches. I did not agree with this, although I did agree that it was important to be separate/sanctified from the world. Young people should **not** be clubbing it up, going to bars, drinking, taking drugs, smoking, lying, fornicating, or living in a world with no distinctions. I believe that truly saved people should have a quality that distinguishes them from the world and mainstream society's lifestyles. I believe that it is important to be baptized in the Holy spirit, as evidenced by speaking in other tongues (Acts 2:4). Baptism in the name of the Lord Jesus Christ for the remission of sins is a key component of the born-again experience, according to (Acts 2:38).

However, (Romans 10:9) is equally important and left out of the Oneness Pentecostal plan for salvation. I believe that it is far more important to have the fruit of the spirit mentioned in (Galatians 5:22–23), which reads, "But the fruit of the spirit is love, joy, peace, longsuffering, gentleness, goodness, faith, meekness, temperance: against such, there is no law." The tongues that we speak should lead to the manifested fruit mentioned in Galatians 5, without it we are wasting our time. As the Apostle Paul said in (1 Corinthians 13:1), "If I speak in the tongues of men and angels, but have not love, I am only a resounding gong or a clanging cymbal." Truly, there was something in me that knew that, although this "Holiness" lifestyle meant well and seemed appealing to my 19–20-year-old mind, it contrasted starkly with what I grew up with within my very first church. I knew that it was somewhat extreme. It seemed that the harder people tried to live a very restricted life, the more they probably struggled with deep, hidden sin. Although I truly believe that many of the old saints and mothers were striving to live holy lives with apostolic truth, their rigidity caused them to lose many people during a certain period in the church's recent history.

I briefly dated a young man who was deep in the ministry at a church I had attended. I met him when I was much younger and did not know that he or his family were highly involved members of the congregation. When I joined, I recognized this young man from an academic institution that I had attended many years prior. Upon recognizing him, I reintroduced myself to this man, whom I had not seen for many years, and asked whether we could get together to catch up on life. In my naiveté I did not realize that the holiness crowd was not accustomed to a woman being platonically "cool" and asking for a phone number simply to catch up with an old friend and that this may have been interpreted as a "come on." It was good to connect with this brother and hear that he was doing well, but soon after, he wanted to "date," while I just wanted to hang out and catch up, even though he was very cute. After congregants saw me with him, they told me that he had a girlfriend and that I needed to "be careful." I ignored this at first because I wanted my friend to tell me the truth and did not plan to interfere with his life. However, I was taken advantage of because I did not know everything and was the new kid on the block. Although I did not want to get caught up in his drama, he began to take off with his girlfriend right in front of me with no explanation. I never slept with this man or fornicated with him. I do not believe in fornicating with someone, then joining the choir and acting as if nothing had happened, or standing in the pulpit as if nothing was going on. I would have been convicted. If I failed to obey God or misstepped outside of the church, I would never return to the church to fool the people. You can't fool bonafide, Holy Ghost-filled ministers and church mothers anyway.

Instead, I would have stepped down until things were right with God. Ultimately, I was not going to be emotionally bounced around like a yoyo. I finally met the other young lady, spoke to her over the phone a few times, and even met her for prayer to let her know that I had no issue with either one of them. My objective was to avoid interfering with whatever they had going on. However, the man formally introduced me to his parents, which was misleading. He wouldn't let me go, even though he still held onto her because she was more familiar. I felt like he was looking for a substitute for her, and I will never be anyone's "side chick." So, I asked my father to give him a call, assuming that he would be reasonable and firm. However, my father did not like to see his daughter getting played, and he wasn't very cordial. Although this incident created a bad situation, I appreciated the result, which ended the mistreatment. I asked for forgiveness for any ill feelings, and that was that. I then became very discouraged that men who were known fornicators were allowed to carry on and participate in ministry, despite showing little or no devotion to Jesus Christ. As a woman, if I had conducted myself like this, I would have been treated very differently. I was burning up and seething, mad that this behavior was ALLOWED to continue while nobody said a word.

Finally, someone spoke from the pulpit, and I thank God for that message because, while it may have rebuked others, it was a blessing to me. When the enemy of my soul found a crack in my armor, people tried to step in and help, but I had to appear strong and shrug off any appearance of hurt for the sake of my dignity. Too many people knew my business, even though they meant well. This situation led me to a great awakening and a disdain for the church. I did not leave that church because of hurt feelings over a lost relationship, but I did not agree with the organization on some significant doctrinal points. Nor did I agree with their position on the role of women in ministry. I believe that God can use a woman to preach, but she should not have a more dominant role than her husband if she's married (1 Timothy 2:12). God does have a divine order where "the head of every man is Christ, and the head of the wife is the man just as the head of Christ is God" (1 Corinthians 11:3). This realization was huge for me, and although many people thought that I was troubled by something as trivial as relationship issues, it was so much deeper. As much as I loved and respected the organization and its leadership, I had big problems with certain aspects of their doctrine and could no longer pretend that those issues did not bother me. We must "worship God in Spirit and truth," according to (John 4:24).

Soon after, I met a young man into "the Nubian Islamic Hebrews or Ansar Allah Community." This brother was standing on the block in Queens with conscious-looking books while I was getting off the train. I approached when he beckoned me and said that I was familiar with his materials. He said I was wrong—that this group wasn't the same anymore but was now called the Holy Tabernacle Ministries or HTM. I had a great conversation with him and wanted to stay in touch because his conversation was intellectually challenging and full of "new" information. I saw him again and continued to pursue a friendship; he reminded me of Quest Love from The Roots, and I thought that was cool at the time. I still felt disconnected from my church and was slowly drifting, even though I was still attending. I was not Biblically illiterate; in fact, I had a good foundational knowledge of the Bible and knew how to witness and teach people but had not learned about apologetics or how to defend the Bible against false doctrine. Although my interaction with this young man was very brief, the impact was damaging, as it opened up a door that could not easily be closed.

His questioning of my faith made me doubt what I believed when both he and my professor at Queensborough Community College (QCC) showed me ancient Sumerian literature that pre-dated the Bible. These two men had no connection, but I believed that they were sent into my life with the same message about the "plagiaristic" nature of the Bible. My teacher at QCC argued that Sargon was Moses and Tammuz (or Damuzi) was a Jesus figure who died and was resurrected. He taught me that Utnapishtim (in the Epic of Gilgamesh) was a "Noah" figure who pre-dated the Bible by thousands of years. It is also theorized the whole Jesus story was derived from much older stories of fertility gods and goddesses. This professor taught us that there was no heaven or hell and that the earlier sky god was Anu; Enki (or Pazuzu), the first Satan character, also predated the Bible. This new information was very troubling, and a few people left this professor's class because their faith was challenged. I stopped coming to class because his presentations caused me great anguish, in addition to what my new boyfriend was "teaching" me. The enemy had double-teamed me, and most Christians would have been unprepared. Even Abraham was a Chaldean from the land of Ur; for this reason (the professor rationalized), the father of the Jews was probably a Chaldean, who worshipped the gods of Mesopotamia before his revelation involving YAHWEH. Many people who embrace these theories assume that if an event comes first historically, anything that happens later must be a stolen story; this sounds logical, but it is not necessarily true. My newfound boyfriend and Ancient Civilization class instructor believed similar things. Although brief, my relationship with this young man was very destructive and quickly terminated. Moving forward, I decided to stop attending church and underwent a cultural and spiritual rebirth. This might seem strange to the average Christian or religious person, but I began to investigate how to cleanse my body, soul, and Spirit. I began to read the Bible again, explore various cultural books, and learn how to serve God from an African theological perspective. I cut off all my relaxed hair and let it grow naturally. I began to buy natural-food cookbooks and found a health-food store in my neighborhood called "Good N Natural." I began to allow the Spirit of God to teach me what to eat during that season of my life. I guess the Church would understand this new diet to be similar to the Daniel Fast, except my diet was a long-term choice and not a twenty-one-day fast. I loved being away from the church and grew closer to God in a glorious way. I was twenty-two and free to be me. I began to wear head wraps, locked my hair for the first time, wore afrocentric jewelry, and became involved in community activism. Social activism was a new call from God in my life, telling me to fight for the oppressed. As (Luke 4:18) says, "The spirit of the LORD is upon me, for he has anointed me to bring good news to the poor. He has sent me to proclaim that captives will be released, that the blind will see, that the oppressed will be set free," I began to attend rallies in New York City with Al Sharpton. My first real rally was in 1997, after a trip to the Nassau Bahamas with my mother. After five days, I came home, went downtown the next day, and rallied for Abner Louima, a Haitian man who was brutally attacked by the police in a bathroom in New York. They took a plunger and inserted it into various parts of his body. Afterward, he needed dental care and internal surgery. This case caused an outrage that lasted for quite a while; Abner Louima subsequently won a multimillion-dollar lawsuit, with damages awarded to him by the city of New York.

Scriptural Nugget: Hebrews 10:38, NLT
"And my righteous ones will live by faith. But I will take no pleasure in anyone who turns away."

Afrocentric Liberation

Fast forward to the late 1990s. I made a vow that I would no longer date Christian men because I saw so much pretense and phoniness in them. I believed that I would find more authenticity from someone who was into something pro-Black, conscious, and spiritual, but not church-related. I heard that more Christian marriages ended in divorce than secular marriages. I also learned that some Black churches do not help Black women find husbands; in fact, one's chances of being single and alone for life were statistically greater at a Black church. While rallying and riding with Sister's Place in Brooklyn, a café/meeting place for the movement, I accompanied activist, Erica Ford. I protested with the December 12th Movement, thanks to a co-worker's commitment to the struggle and liberation of Black people. A sister on my job invited me to various meetings and rallies and encouraged me to continue within the mantle of activism and revolutionary thought. I took this consciousness very seriously, as my parents had embraced a 1960s pro-Black revolutionary approach to our plight as people. As I was now in my early twenties, I was able to participate freely.

In 1996, I attended the one-year anniversary of the Million Man March (The Day of Atonement) in New York City, hosted by Minister Louis Farrakhan. It was wonderful to be in his presence. In 1998, I attended the Million Woman's March in Philadelphia, hosted by Jada Pinkett Smith, and then, later that year, the Million Youth March with the late Dr. Khalid Abdul Muhammad. He was greatly feared by the establishment and died in mysterious circumstances in 2001. At this point in my life, I had felt that I had been lied to on so many levels. I still read my Bible from time to time, and I certainly still prayed. I could still feel the presence of the Holy Spirit, for which I gave praise and thanks. I was very, very happy because I felt that my life as an activist had meaning and purpose. I took part in social justice and civil-rights activities that made me feel like I was truly giving back to the world. This practice felt less confining than contributing to the church. I read more cultural books and studied holistic health books by some greats, including Laila Afrika and Queen Afua. These books delved deeply into teaching holistic health and vegan/vegetarianism as a lifestyle. Finally, I was free from the traditional church's restrictions and realized that I could be free as a Black woman in my spiritual expression, without the artificial feeling that I sometimes had in church. Although I always loved and adored church, I still feel that the expectations caused people to behave in authentic ways. In the church, there is a lot of personality repression. As one African spirituality teacher said, the church is often a flawed behavior-shaping system; it may reform behaviors for a little while, but the transformation does not seem to stick for many people. Those who have had a truly redemptive, born-again experience can say that the saving power of Jesus Christ has transformed them. However, some people choose to evolve, change, grow, and shift into a deeper understanding of who Christ is. When I go to church, why should I have to stop being an African American woman who loves her Africanness and enjoys wearing African jewelry, ankhs, and African symbols that Eurocentric, Westernized Christian thought may deem sinful and pagan?

I am sorry, but I do not agree with this thought process. As the Scripture states, "There is neither Greek, not Jew nor male or female" (Galatians 3:28). Even though the ability to celebrate culture and identity has nothing to do with belief, people may use it to diminish the importance of ethnic diversity, culture, and the differences that make humans unique and beautiful. I learned that my spiritual identity in Christ did not mean that I had to become a neutralized Black woman, unable to celebrate the culture God gave me when He created me. Many African descendants who consider themselves conscious do not identify as Christian because they have been taught that Christianity is a Eurocentric, White-man's religion. Many in the conscious Black community are not interested in the character named "Jesus," even going so far as to question a historical Jesus's existence. Those in the conscious community make a very strong case for being anti-Jesus; anger derived from their upbringing has made them hate Jesus because he represents oppression and not liberation. Also, he does not offer a positive cultural identity because (in their minds) people who want to be more like

God have to be more White. Since early European Christians acted as missionaries in West Africa during colonial and slave-trading times, many people in the conscious Black community assume no Christian presence on the African continent before western colonialism. However, research shows that this is not true at all. Christianity appeared in Coptic settings in ancient Egypt and Ethiopia before the establishment of the Catholic Church. The Eunuch in the book of Acts (Chapter 8: 26–40) encounters the Apostle Phillip, who baptizes him when he has heard the Gospel of Jesus Christ. According to Ethiopian legends, The Eunuch later returned to Ethiopia and reported back to the Kendake Queen. This story is just one account of Christianity in early African culture. There are many other examples of Christianity in Africa before the European presence.

During this time of cultural self-discovery, I found out that my paternal grandmother was going to Orangeburg, South Carolina, her hometown. I saw this as a wonderful opportunity to find out about my father's family and their South Carolina lineage. I rode a Greyhound bus (never again!) with my grandmother, aunt, and younger cousins; this trip seemed to take between thirteen and sixteen hours. I did not enjoy the smelly stops, smelly bus, and distinct caliber of people trying to travel to various destinations in the best way. I was exhausted. En route, I discovered that we would stay with my father's half-sister's aunt, who was the sister of her biological father. This woman was also related by marriage to some of the leaders from the GRT church! I could not believe that we were related through marriage. My aunt and the gentlemen I had dated shared the same first cousin but were not related by blood. I discovered that the sibling of the church leader married my paternal grandmother's sister-in-law.

The trip was an enlightening experience, but I became the object of verbal and emotional abuse, which my father warned could happen. That experience was truly horrible, and I vowed never to subject myself to such treatment again. I understand why my father was broken after enduring an environment that was hostile on many levels. To reduce the pain, sorrow, and sadness of the experience, he self-medicated with alcohol to treat his depression. Sadly, both my parents endured this type of treatment from people who should have loved and protected them. I truly believe that their parents loved them, but their mothers were scorned and betrayed by the men they loved and had children with. It has to hurt deeply when the man you love does not honor or respect you enough to marry you—or, in the case of my maternal grandmother—the man you love and the father of your only child has affairs and conceals the birth of a child outside of marriage. Past negative experiences do not excuse bad behavior; we should identify such behavior and cut it off at the root. However, both of my grandmothers raised two children who subconsciously believed that dysfunction was normal. They accepted it and took very few preventive measures to prevent their idiosyncrasies from continuing into the next generation. What people deem normal can damage our offspring if we do not take the time to come into the saving knowledge of Jesus and allow Him to heal and deliver us from our pain. God wants us to give Him the pieces of our broken lives because He has fashioned our hearts, and we are the clay in the potter's hands, as mentioned in (Jeremiah 18:1-4). If we depend completely on the master's hands, things may progress at a better pace in our spiritual lives. In 1998, after my year of Afrocentric blossoming, my grandmother's health went into a deep and final decline. Of course, I was terrified. Her seizures reappeared and got worse, and her medication no longer worked to control them.

In November 1998, I moved to Brooklyn and was happy, trying to live my life. On separate occasions, my parents came to visit me there. My mom came through like she was Diahann Carol (a very prissy Black woman style) and had the nerve to ask me why I did not have a doorman like they do in Manhattan. Looking back, I suspect she really liked the area and the brownstone with the bay windows; alternatively, perhaps she was envious of my freedom. I was twenty-three years old, with no roommate or boyfriend, and free at last. I had a very lucrative fly-by-night position at a company called Schick Technologies, where I was making 4,000 dollars a month, which wasn't bad at all for someone my age with no degree. However, I could sense that this company might go under.

I worried that at least my department would go under because we were making way too much money. My father warned me that it was simply too good to be true. I then got terribly sick with the flu and had to stay home for a few days. My mother said, "with all the money that you make, you don't get sick pay?" I said I didn't, and she said, "well, that's not a good job." At that age, I didn't know much about insurance or paid time off, and

I was anti-system, anti-government, and anti-everything. However, she was right. She then used fear against me, telling me that my grandmother's health declined and she did not know how much longer she had to live. This fear tactic worked. I did not know whether my job was stable and, a few months later, my department closed down, followed by the closure of the company two years later. A year before that, I had gone on my first trip abroad, to the Bahamas with my mother. This moment was a life-changing, wonderful trip, where I felt rejuvenated and went to another level of consciousness as a Black and spiritual young woman. Leaving the church, full of hurt and confusion, was empowering, on the one hand, because I discovered things about myself culturally and created change as an activist (or so I believed).

I found myself seeking the Nuwaupians and those in HTM. I wanted more information to satisfy and justify my need to be angry and oppose the church and everyone in it. I traveled all the way to Bushwick Brooklyn from the Bronx on Sunday afternoons to hear the word of the Holy Tabernacle Ministries under the auspices of Dr. Malachi Z. York. In fact, I swapped one church for the other. I began to regularly attend these "Right Knowledge" classes in 1998 and used to see these "brothers" who came to class joyfully with their friends. I didn't think much of them at the time, but I liked their unity, enthusiasm, and innocent belief in Dr. York's teachings. I never spoke to them, but I met great young women I loved to spend time with. This class's information was so fantastic that I would ponder all I had learned about various world religions and everything else that you had questions about that the church could not and did not dare to answer. After these classes, a nice meal would be served for a small donation. We sat around and talked and got to know one another. It was truly a beautiful thing, seeing young Generation-Xers in our twenties who were thirsty for this "new" spiritual knowledge and also loved ourselves and each other on a deeper level, as young Black people united for a "cause." Certainly, there were a few elders; older people were available to teach and instruct. I loved seeing a strong sister (as I thought at the time) teach the classes in a sharp, no-nonsense manner.

After attending the tabernacle meetings consistently for almost a year, one of the young men who went around with his younger brothers and their best friend greeted me by saying, "Hey gorgeous." I was extremely turned off by this, which should have made me realize that we were not equally yoked from day one. I never liked to be admired for my physical appearance alone. I said peace to him, spoke briefly, and kept things moving. He seemed to have been through hard times and a lifestyle that might not have been completely righteous. This summation turned out not to be completely true—I was judging the book by its cover. However, after some time had passed, I began to see the sweetness in him. I classified this meeting as a brief encounter and did not expect it to go anywhere.

In the summer of 1998, much of the crew went to Tama-Re, a place built in the town of Eatonton, Georgia. After some fundraising, Dr. York erected an Egyptian-style compound with pyramid structures and Egyptian statues, which surrounded the park with a continuous Om chant that was very hypnotic. As a matter of fact, it was quite demonic, and my Spirit was deeply disturbed. Other Om chants never made me feel this way, but this one was dark; it was also in Dr. York's voice. Everything was about Dr. York: the songs, the meditations, the books, the messages, everything. These are telltale signs of a cult. In the classic sense, York's followers saw him as God. His divinity was unquestioned. If you dissented or saw things differently, you were shunned. If you disagreed with the doctrine, you were against either "the master teacher" or "the lamb." The books, materials, and name of the organization constantly changed. The organization's name changed several times, from the Ansar Allah Community to the Nubian Islamic Hebrews, Holy Tabernacle Ministries, United Nuwaupian Nation of Moors, The Nuwaubians, AEO, and Ancient Egyptian Order of Melchizedek to Washitaw Nation, and finally The Sabaens (2019). The name could change at any moment if he got tired of that particular school of thought. I began talking to my then-future (now ex-) husband as a friend. I wasn't attracted to him until I got to know his personality, which was really caring. As time went on, he became more proactive. He started talking to me after he came back from his trip to Tama-Re in Georgia. I had seen pictures and was not overly impressed with what I'd seen, but if you've never traveled very far and all you know lies within a twenty-mile radius, then you might have thought that Tama-Re was something very special. Although I wasn't impressed to that extent, I was "down" for anything that appeared to help Black people escape from Western society and have their own. When I was older and wiser, I learned that no one could separate from society within a society. If you want your nation, you must build it somewhere else or declare war on the dominant society. Realistically, you probably don't have the armed forces or manpower to overthrow the dominant culture. Over the next couple of months, I continued to attend classes. By the end of the year, the young man and I exchanged numbers and became friends. He said that he would be moving into the Tabernacle and giving up his life for the Nuwaupian Nation agenda. I thought this was noble—evidence of some sort of pure-hearted devotion. I moved into my first apartment in Brooklyn to be closer to the organization, get away from all that I had known, and grow.

As soon as I arrived in Brooklyn, my new friend told me that the Brooklyn chapter would be moving closer to the area I had left, in Mount Vernon, New York. Although this was problematic, I wanted to get closer to my new friend, and my mother had scared me into returning to the Bronx by saying that my grandmother didn't have long to live and someone needed to take care of "her mother," as I had always done. This situation was very troubling initially, but eventually, I began to think that this was by divine design. My new potential love called me daily, and we became close friends. When he propagated in Harlem with another member of the organization, they would set up a table and sell books directly across the street from GRT while talking to people passing in the street. A twisted part of me wanted GRT to see me out there with him, and some of them did. Sometimes I stopped by to assist him. People were being used in all five boroughs to raise money for the organization. Some did this independently to make a daily personal living, but those who lived inside the organization made no money of their own. My boyfriend needed a way out and did not want that life because the living conditions were deplorable. My home soon became a place he could visit, take showers, and be comfortable. My grandmother had a daytime home-health aide, and I was out of a job, knowing my grandmother did not have long to live. Needing the security of a family, I thought, why not start a family of my own? I was about to lose one of the most important figures in my entire life, and I had a boyfriend with a large family that seemed close-knit. So, we spent more time together and became lovers. After nine months of knowing him, I got pregnant on purpose. It wasn't an accident, as my mother thought. I wanted a child, and three months later, we got married. My mother insisted that I terminate the pregnancy or marry him so that she would not be shamed by my having a child out of wedlock. Although she tried to scare me into doubting my ability to be a parent, I kept my baby. Again, the spirit of manipulation and control was at work. However, I was twenty-four and old enough to make an informed decision. Both of us were jobless since I had recently resigned from my job, given the company's instability. However, I began to work for Temp agencies. As my husband did not have a job, we (my family) fought to find him one because he had a child on the way. The reality of his responsibilities made him hostile. Even the leaders at his organization said that he should try to make it on his own with his family. Shortly after becoming pregnant, I had renounced all ties with Nuwaupians and returned to an Assembly of God church. When Donnie Mcclurkin's *"We Fall Down, But We Get Up"* debuted on TBN, I watched and wept. This song truly put me back on the path toward Christ.

When I went back to church with my baby growing inside of me, I had emotional support and rededicated myself. The shift angered my husband, who believed that I was as attached to the Nuwaupian cult as he was. However, I had seen its true inner workings and realized that this was not where I needed to be. When people claimed that the statues were moving on Tama-Re while they were meditating and that York was an alien messianic figure, I renounced these beliefs and got out of the cult as quickly as I had gotten in. I made a vow to the Lord never to go to another Nuwaupian event, and I never did. With my good AG church's support, I regained my spiritual footing and got centered on Christ as my baby was coming into the world. The church was even nice enough to throw me a baby shower, which my mother did not bother to do. My mother tried to make the situation difficult for me, and she later regretted this. When I could no longer work, I had to quit my temporary job. By then, my husband was working at Saks Fifth Avenue doing odd jobs. This role helped him to break into the adult workforce. He had previously held typical teen jobs, where I had held more clerical positions in office settings. This period in my life was a serious struggle because I had never experienced anything like this. At the last minute, my mother and husband came through, and I had everything I needed. Why she tortured me like that, I don't know. However, she secretly told one of her girlfriends that she would make things difficult for me by offering very little support so that I would "feel it." My baby was scheduled due during the first week of December 1999. However, God had a different plan, and so did my child. My son, whose gender was known in July 1999, was causing painful contractions. I endured them for about three days because my water had not broken, and I wanted to be sure that I was crowning and not having false labor. Although I had pulled my mucous plug, nothing that splashed out soaked me, so I did not realize that my water had broken.

In the early morning of Thanksgiving Day, I thought my child was going to explode through my rear end instead of using the normal exit for babies. It was clearly time to go to the hospital and deliver this baby, as Macy's Thanksgiving Day Parade was on TV. I had been looking forward to good food and a wonderful Thanksgiving feast, but there was something much more fulfilling on the way, and that was my child. We called an ambulance, and two women arrived. They took us to the hospital, where I delivered my baby after six hours of prep. My mother was there with her husband, and my beloved father hopped on a Metro-North train from upstate New York on a holiday schedule, got out of town on the earliest train he could get and made it to the Bronx two hours before I delivered. When my father arrived, I knew that I could do this. Of course, my husband was there too. After an epidermal, I delivered my baby boy and named him Ayinde, a Nigerian name that means "we gave praises, and he came." I named my son after a young boy (Ayinde Jean Baptiste), who had spoken powerfully at the Million Man March four years prior. I wanted my son to have his namesake's powerful attributes and a name with some cultural/spiritual meaning. I cried, my father cried, and my husband cried. My father left about an hour later, and my mother was allowed back into the room. I had previously asked her to leave because she was too anxious and wanted to control the doctors and my way of delivering my baby. I needed cool, level-headed people with focused energy in the room. Man, I was hungry after the delivery and very upset to have missed Thanksgiving dinner, but oh so happy to be a brand-new mother of a beautiful baby boy.

I truly believe that God gave me a quick and beautiful vision of my son's life. Before he was born, God gave me a vision of what he would look like at the age of one, when my son was one, how he looked just as he appeared in the dream. In the dream, he was talking like a grown-up. However, just after my son was born in the hospital, I had a vision in quick succession in his early years, from that moment to the age of eighteen. With tears in my eyes, I began to pray over every year of his life that I was shown and onward to the years I did not see. My son was circumcised and passed his meconium. I started producing milk and nursed him for the first time in the hospital. I began to feel claustrophobic and paranoid as I waited for someone to pick us up as my husband was getting the house ready. I was having a hormonal drop and beginning to feel depressed and anxious about being a new mother. This feeling was only temporary; as soon as my hormones normalized, being a new mother became a joy. We came home, and reality sunk in that we were parents. Then the fun began, along with the challenges.

Financially, we were ill-prepared, but I got everything that I needed, with my family and husband's help. I stayed home for three months and enjoyed bonding with my son. I grew in prayer as a mother, constantly praying about my son's life. I prayed for every scenario I could imagine in my child's life, and I loved spending time with him, nursing him, holding him, and talking to him. Eventually, after three months, it was time to return to work. I had found a job in Jersey City, not too far from the World Trade Center. The firm was called Georgeson Shareholder, and I worked as a customer-service agent there for about six months. Daily travel was a difficult journey, as I had to get up early in the cold, store breast milk for my son, and commute for nearly two hours to get to work. My mother and husband took turns taking care of my son, while my husband also continued to work. I hated leaving my son—it broke my heart.

However, I had to keep a roof over his head. After a while, this job became easier. I trusted my mom and was thankful for her involvement. I was no longer involved in anything Nuwaupian and never returned to an affiliated event. I made a vow to God because I saw nothing deeply spiritual in that organization—just heady, high-minded, intellectual pursuits. I never worshipped Dr. York, or thought he was an extraterrestrial, believed that his doctrine was unique or exceptionally profound, or thought that Tama-Re was stunningly impressive. I enjoyed reading other Black authors and lacked the Yorkian cult mentality. I never thought that York was the only answer for the entire Black race.

Of course, I was happy to see Black people striving to build and do different things. I loved much of the information and books. I learned a lot but knew how to take the meat and spit out the bones. However, Ayinde's dad was highly impressed and obviously got something out of that organization that he felt significantly changed him for the better over the years. In 2000, a group of Nuwaupians we knew really well-traveled home from Tama-Re, in Georgia. According to reports, the group wanted to get back to New York quickly; they were driving at night and going about 90 miles per hour. They met with an accident in which two of our friends were killed; other people that we knew suffered very bad injuries but survived. For me, this was confirmation: when God says to leave something, he makes it easy and crystal clear (2 Corinthians 6:17). It could have been our family in that vehicle, as my son's father lived among those people and could have traveled with that group on organizational business. Although I wept, I was clear and fully aware that God had His hand in this. I was spared because the Holy Spirit still operated in my life; even though I had moved to the left, I still belonged to God.

My husband was verbally and emotionally abusive. At times, he was even physically aggressive, grabbing my arms and pointing fingers in my face. The abuse caused me to retaliate because I am not the type to take things lying down. In the beginning, his behavior used to hurt deeply and disturb me, making me cry. The abuse began with my husband calling me a "motherfucker" when I was pregnant. No one had ever called me this before. On top of this, I was carrying his child. He seemed unaware of the vibratory frequency he was sending both of us, even though he claimed to have "Right Knowledge" and the great teachings of Dr. York. I was never going to follow or submit to him as a leader in any capacity; when a man presents himself as temperamentally out of control, his behavior is the opposite of what women respect, controlled, refined masculinity. Sadly, this behavior continued. Our parenting styles were completely different, and my husband was not nurturing with our son. He simply did not understand the emotional sacrifice needed when people become parents, and he was not equipped emotionally to make such a sacrifice. The positive aspects of my husband's parenting style involved being consistent, loyal, and actively present. Those aren't enough, unfortunately. He was the sort of parent who thinks that it's enough to provide for their children financially, without considering their spiritual, emotional, or intellectual development. Our domestic disputes escalated into public embarrassment, as he blamed me for his outbursts, cursed at me on the street, and started public arguments. Public dysfunction was not my style and not how I was raised. However, I have an eyewitness account that he may have been raised like this. Having seen such behavior as a child, he probably thought that screaming and cursing on the street was an acceptable way to have a disagreement. I never behaved like this, and nor did my mother, grandmother, or great-grandmother. If my father was aggressive when he was drunk, I never witnessed it. However, even though I never witnessed domestic violence among my own relatives, my mother allowed my stepfather to abuse me.

Although he never beat me black and blue, he shoved me, roughed me up, and jumped in my face, threatening to hurt me. My mother did not make him stop. Fortunately, I was only exposed to such behavior for four months, but that was long enough to imprint negative grooves in my fourteen-to-fifteen-year-old mind. I believed that I had worked through these issues and been delivered from their influence, but perhaps it wasn't enough since I married a man who thought he could do the same to me. At least, he learned quickly. My mother noticed immediately that my ex-husband was abusive and finally said when my son was nine months old, "Lori, I think he is abusive, and you need to let him go. He is out of control, and this is not good for your child." I agreed with her, and she said she would support me in any way she could—I would not be alone and should not tolerate this. So, I threw my husband out and began raising my son alone. I also applied for a new job that was listed in the *New York Times*. This position drew on my cosmetology education, as the state-licensed me as a cosmetologist. The job was at Clairol, now owned by Proctor and Gamble, and it was my first really enjoyable high-end job. I had previously had "high-end" and "prestigious" internships, which allowed me to work with high-profile people at an exclusive salon, Salon Ishi in Manhattan, which charged wealthy people 200–500 dollars for a haircut. However, this job was the perfect opportunity to use my cosmetology training, customer service skills, and latent counseling skills by helping people solve color correction issues involving green, purple, or pink hair over the phone. Although I enjoyed many aspects of this job, I had a very mean supervisor, who seemed nice at first, but quickly flipped once she learned that the company was going under. Nevertheless, it was a great experience. I developed high-level professional skills and was proud to say that I worked for a well-known hair-care institution. A year later, the company was bought out, and its employees were relocated to Connecticut; it later outsourced to Mexico. I decided to jump ship before everything hit the fan. For one thing, having fallen very sick on the job one day, sitting directly under the air conditioner and choking on my own mucous, I discovered that my boss had no empathy. It was time to go, and rightfully so. At the same time, I was completing a BA in Psychology at the College of New Rochelle. Some good, positive, and well-educated Rastas inspired me to return to my studies, and I thank God for that. One of the Rasta sisters already had her Master's degree and worked at a very elite and renowned institution in New York. A Rasta brother, who was completing his degree, advised me to go back to school and use every gift God had given me. I became very motivated and returned to college a few days after 9/11, transferring twelve credits while caring for my almost-two-year-old baby. My mother generally cared for my son at night, with occasional assistance from her current husband. It was very kind of them to do that for me. After I finished this degree, I sought counsel from spiritual elders on the route I should take toward graduate and doctoral degrees. I began to pray, visualize, and meditate on Fordham University's Graduate School of Education program. After researching some of the best programs in New York, I concluded that Fordham University was my only choice for many reasons. I am so thankful for this program, as the experience transformed my life.

After being out of work for a while, I went into the field of E-commerce, which was fairly new at the time; my firm handled the interchange of electronic data between retailers and buyers. I was a customer service rep and making a very nice salary, with great bonuses. I was also treated like royalty by a caring and loving boss. At that job, I received a major bonus of 800–1,000 dollars every month, in addition to my salary. Although this was very welcomed, I knew that something was not right. Why would a thriving company suddenly start giving out tons of cash while removing key people? After a year, a special business consultant came in to warn us that the company was failing. I was eventually downsized with many other people. Fortunately, I received an excellent severance package that supported me for four months while searching for a new job. Just as my severance and unemployment were about to run out, I was called in to interview for a position as a customer service agent for the online *New York Times*. After a second interview, I got the job. It was truly a thrilling and exciting experience. At this point, I was exactly one year into my graduate studies at Fordham University.

Scriptural Nugget: 2 Corinthians 6:14, NLT

"Don't team up with those who are unbelievers. How can righteousness be a partner with wickedness? How can light live with darkness?"

This Can't Be Happening

In late summer 2005, my mother was diagnosed with cancer, which had metastasized throughout her body. I immediately became her counselor, pastor, intercessor, and best friend. Two months after my mother received brain surgery to remove cancerous growths, I was diagnosed with fibroids. It was an extremely difficult time, and I spent many sleepless nights praying on the floor for my mother to be healed, and her life to be extended. When I received my own diagnosis, I wept in her arms, feeling defeated. She was still my mom, saying, "this will not happen to you." God bless her always. I prayed for my mother into salvation with the sinner's prayer, and she was finally receptive. Even though she had begun a spiritual path in Unity many years before, I seized the opportunity and found that she was receptive. During this period, I watched my mom grow closer to God and spend two hours a day in devotion and morning worship. Through her efforts, supported by a powerful dose of wheatgrass juice twice a day, she was able to extend her life far beyond what the doctors predicted, which was six months.

When I first heard this news about my mother, the faculty advisors at my school, who were good psychologists, who told me to take time off and come back when I was ready. I did just that and took a semester off for a leave of absence. I broke down and cried in my faculty advisor's office, knowing that I had reached a turning point in my life and would need to draw on all of my spiritual learning in this season. During this dark period, I had supernatural levels of inner strength, which could have only been through the Holy Spirit. "I would have fainted had I not believed that we would see the goodness of the Lord in the land of the living." (Psalm 27:13). I pulled on God and cried out to Him. As I became my mother's pastor and life coach during the first year, I watched both of us grow. After one semester off, I returned to school with delayed graduation. My constant prayer was, "Lord, I dedicate this work to my mother. Please don't let her leave this life before I graduate." Every other night, with no chemo or radiation therapy, my mother faithfully took care of my son so that I could go to graduate-school classes at night at the Fordham Graduate School of Education Lincoln Center Campus in Manhattan. Time progressed, my mother continued her deep devotions, and I got an internship at the John Jay College of Criminal Justice counseling center with the mentor I wanted. I graduated successfully with an A average My mother did not expect me to do something inconceivable to her, even though we had discussed it for more than a year: I decided to reconcile with my ex-husband and relocate to Georgia after completing my Masters degree. My mother felt that she was dying and I was abandoning her, which I never did. Under duress, my mother remarried her ex-husband for financial support, including the health insurance she needed. I warned my mother and advised her that she was not alone, given that she had a previous husband in her life to help take care of her.

Between 1995 and 2007, I avidly watched Bishop Long on the Trinity Broadcasting Network. When the internet became more advanced, I watched Long's New Birth services in Georgia live on *"Streaming Faith,"* on the New Birth website. Those messages confirmed everything for me. Bishop Eddie Long looked into the camera and said, "some of you are watching me online right now, and God told you to move to Georgia because I am your Pastor, and this is your church home." Bishop Long did a whole series on breaking free from old mindsets and embracing new thoughts, explaining that our families and parents may have meant well but instilled in us some false beliefs. Long stayed on this series, which focused on uprooting oneself to achieve a new beginning. My mother was active, with no chemo or radiation. She was not in bed or wasting away. Mommy was doing wonderfully and had her husband to support and care for her. Although he was usually at her house, she felt reluctant to have him as a full-time husband. I did not understand this reunion, and I found it very strange. In 2006, my mother was still vibrant. We had taken a wonderful six-day trip to St. Lucia in the West Indies to see the Jazz Festival during Mother's Day weekend, where we saw legendary jazz and R&B artists, including Al Green, Nancy Wilson, and

Kenneth Babyface Edmonds. We met these three either in our hotel lobby or on the beach. I still think it's wonderful that I got to relax for two days in a row on the beach with Babyface. Too bad that the Smart Phone wasn't out yet—I would have had some fabulous celebrity pictures. My mother and I had a great time together, and one afternoon, in a hot tub at the hotel spa, my mom had a breakthrough. She apologized, cried, and said she was sorry for being hypercritical and hard on me. She knew that she had always wanted to be perfect and set that perfectionism trap for me. She acknowledged that it was not fair. I forgave her, and we both cried in that Jacuzzi-style hot tub at the Spa in St. Lucia. She gave me a piece of what I wanted to hear but never admitted that she had sacrificed her daughter for her satisfaction. The tragedy was that she never got what she wanted or expected from the relationship. Our six days in St Lucia passed quickly and, before I knew it, we were back in New York. I returned to class, applied for an internship in counseling and higher education, which I successfully obtained, and completed my Master of Science in Education and Counseling at Fordham University. The tremendous thing was that my mother MADE IT all the way to graduation, which was my prayer to God. I felt that receiving a Master's degree was the greatest gift I could give my mother to thank her for all that she tried to do for me by sacrificing so much so that I could go to private school and obtained the best education. The least I could do was to show her that all of it was all worth it since she had worried about me.

For many years, I looked like I might not make it; this was a way to redeem myself. Besides, I wanted to give something back and help others, just as I was helped by people who intervened when I was younger. To date, I have no regrets about my Fordham University journey. That academic experience changed my life for the better and instilled in me a confidence that I could be effective and competent, even in the most emotionally strenuous and devastating situations. When I told my mother that I was reconciling with my ex-husband in Georgia, she did not want me to leave. He had lost his home through a predatory lender and expected me to drop everything and save his house, even though we were divorced. Granted, it was truly a beautiful home, but he had no furniture and was living off a blow-up bed when I visited. When I visited Loganville, Georgia, with our son, I wished that I could stay and make something of this house, which had so much great potential. However, I could not stay, as we were no longer married, and he never consulted with me on the house when he bought it, merely seeking my help with the mortgage when his predatory loan kicked in, and the payments got too high. I was still in graduate school, finishing my Master's degree, when he asked me to transfer and move to Georgia to help him out of a jam. Of course, I told him that this was impossible, as I was no longer his wife. I told him that my graduate degree credits could not be transferred to other programs, and internships are often a once-in-a-lifetime deal. I had everything lined up for my degree program's final year, and my mother was six months into her stage-four cancer diagnosis. How dare he ask me for help! Instead, he asked his brother to give up a few months to help him get back on his feet and save the house from foreclosure. I advised him to refinance or seek a second job to make up the difference. Instead of listening, he did neither, abandoning the house, letting it be foreclosed, and filing for bankruptcy. Had we been married, I doubt any of this would have happened. I think he could have found a way to refinance, but fear in a faithless person can shut down blessings before they materialize.

Months passed, and I was deeply involved in my externship as a counselor and academic advisor, where I had my first opportunity of teaching at the college level. This graduate externship was life-changing, enabling me to discover my professional identity and recognize my gifts. I am thankful to God for this opportunity and experience, as they were truly transformational. Finally, after holding my breath for nearly two years with hope and desperate prayers, my mother lived to see me graduate with a Master's degree from Fordham University's Graduate School of Education. During this time, I devoutly watched Bishop Eddie Long on *"Streaming Faith"* live online. His message about leaving old mindsets and unhealthy familial patterns were so on point that I knew it was time to leave New York. The Holy Spirit began to nudge me, confirming over and over that I needed to be in the house of New Birth, being taught by Bishop Long, who so accurately preached about where my heart was and where I was trying to go. I was transformed by what I was hearing. The externship period was difficult because I had quit my job at the *New York Times* and had taken an unpaid internship. My prayer life had gone through the roof, between my mother's condition and my lack of money, which forced me to depend on the system (something no member of my mother's family ever did) while supporting my son and myself. I saw God make something out of nothing. So many miracles took place during my time of need. Provisions were always there, and my prayer life intensified. I knew I would need a lot of faith for the next journey. Finally, the blessed and wonderful day came, after two-and-a-half years of school two nights a week, with my mother caring for my son when she could. I finally graduated with an MS.Ed in Counseling and Personnel Services. I was ready to take on the world and make a positive contribution to society. Although I had tried to prepare my mother for my departure, my parents were devastated when the time came. Before leaving, I visited my father regularly at his home in upstate New York. I wanted my son to spend as much time with him as possible. I am so glad that he did since time is a precious gift that cannot be retrieved once it is gone.

My mother and I wept at the kitchen table on the morning that she asked me to have "the talk" with her. With tears, she said, "I just want to tell you that I give you my blessing on your move to Atlanta, Georgia." I also began to cry and told her that if she could not go to her dream destination of Las Vegas, one of us has to go forward and make a new start. I told her that when she died, there would be nothing left for me in the Bronx. I could not imagine staying in the apartment next door when she wasn't there. I had already lost my grandmother, great-grandmother, and great aunt, who helped raise me in Co-op City, where my parents were divorced in Co-op City. What was left for me? Having consulted and talked to God, I knew deep down inside that I had to start over and build a different, more positive life for my son and myself in a new location. I received intense "word" from the New Birth live stream and the Late Bishop Eddie Long's profound, compelling declarations. They were so relevant, even though he could not have known what I was going through or the change I needed to make. Many people thought that I was wrong to leave or running away from my mother's impending passing, but this was not true. In hindsight, I believe that my mother remarried out of fear and confusion. Her choice made no sense, and I can only pray that I will never be in the same position in my life. My mother chose to remarry someone whom she knew to be a mistake. When I decided to leave, she could function with minimal assistance, even refusing my help and relying more on her husband (whom she did not live with) instead of me. At the time, I tried to be positive and trusted God to restore the situation. However, there were other motives that my mother did not recognize because she was in poor health. When I questioned the circumstances objectively, she refused to listen. My mother stopped listening to the Godly advice that I tried to give her, resuming the same cycle with this man that I witnessed as a teenager. In my own life, I have followed some of her patterns, with better results. The Bible says, "For God has not given us a spirit of fear, but of power and of love and of a sound mind" (2 Timothy 1:7). I have learned that it is bad to remarry ex-husbands because we fear being alone or are not as comfortable economically as we were during the marriage. Once we learn to grow from faith to faith and glory to glory, we trust that God will meet our every need, providing for us when we can't see "the how" in particular situations. As Matthew (6:30) says, "And if God cares so wonderfully for wildflowers that are here today and thrown into the fire tomorrow, he will certainly care for you. Why do you have so little faith?"

I decided to reunite with my ex-husband and join him in Georgia, where I could also have the "New Birth" experience in a new church in the Atlanta region. It turned out to be a time of great spiritual growth, which changed my life and taught me so many things about myself. During my last few months in New York, I saved money, bought an Amtrak train ticket for myself and my son, and packed using supernatural money because I had no income at this time. I hired a professional mover, sold many items, including some that had belonged to my grandmother, and got ready. One day, I went down to the basement in my building to do the laundry, having prayed that God would shut down the opportunity to move to Georgia if it was not His will. I was pressed for time, about to graduate, and had little time, having given notice to the office that managed my property, letting them know that the apartment was for sale. To my surprise, there was a sign in the laundry room, someone wanted to transfer from a one-bedroom apartment to a two-bedroom apartment because they were expecting, and their family was about to expand. I said, "Lord, this can't be real! God is so amazing." The timing was perfect, so I took the information and said that I would call that person during the week. Later, I was wearing my tan "Harv`e Bernard" business skirt suit while waiting for the Express Bus, which, in New York, is a luxurious way to travel to Manhattan. While waiting, my neighbor, an Ethiopian/Eritrean brother whose family I was friendly with, drove up in his Cadillac and said, "do you need a ride?" I said, "sure!" He was working at the UN in Manhattan, and I was doing my externship training. He asked me how I was, and I said, "I'm great and getting ready to move soon, but I need to sell my apartment." He said, "I put a sign up in the laundry." I said, "that was YOU?" He said yes, and I almost shouted in his car: "this is NOBODY but God." We talked and made arrangements, and he invited me for a traditional "Ethio-Eritrean" supper with his family. He then inspected the apartment and said he would take it "as is." I was thrilled, he was thankful, and we celebrated each other's new journeys! His family and his wife were thankful, and I was on my way to Georgia.

At the time, I had no income and had to rely on the system because of my unpaid externship. I felt that this was SHAMEFUL, as I did not have that sort of upbringing, and no one in my family lived like this. It was a situation that could not continue. I sold everything in my house that was old, had value, or had belonged to my grandmother, raising over 500 dollars. I had an appraiser come in to assess and buy her quality bedroom furniture from the early 1960s. My grandmother collected fine china, some of which could be sold. Other items simply had to be given away. I had an outstanding bill from the last semester of graduate school because my loan ran out. However, my mother's husband loaned me the money, and I immediately paid it back with a portion of my income tax return. I used some of my stipends in cash I had saved to pay a professional mover. Then I boxed my own items, bought two Amtrak tickets for my son and myself, and was ready to leave New York.

As the time came to depart, I grew truly excited and wanted to reunite with my ex-husband and try to make our marriage work. I prayed to God and asked Him to help me change if I was too bourgie, too picky, too prim, too mouthy, or too moody. I also asked God to change my ex-husband's verbally abusive behavior and anger issues. I believed that if I changed the things I said and how I responded to him and prayed through hard times like a good wife, he would change. How naive I was. My ex-husband seemed sincerely excited that we were coming back. He phoned us daily from Georgia and sounded warm over the phone. I was thrilled to be leaving New York. With hindsight, was I really following God's call to a new life? Yes, I truly believe I was. The ridiculous confirmations I received after tuning into the Holy Spirit and the messages from the New Birth pulpit were just too strong to ignore. Normally, I would not join a church with "Baptist" in the title, but Long was previously affiliated with the FGBC (Full Gospel Baptist Church) International organization. It was founded by Bishop Paul S. Morton, who believed in many of the same things as Pentecostals. Also, the church leadership is an episcopacy, unlike many traditional Baptist institutions, which still use the incorrect title, "Reverend" (Psalm 111:9, Matthew 23:8-11) and have no ecclesiastical oversight, apart from a local board and possibly the National Baptist Convention, which does not provide a biblical ecclesiastical order for leadership and oversight, as I understand it (see Acts 20:17-28; Acts 21:18, Titus 1:5, Timothy 5: 17-22). The FGBC website has a statement section that lists the *12 Beliefs We Live By*. These are very similar to the Apostolic Pentecostal beliefs, minus the oneness aspect, which is fine with me.

Holiness and the focus on the Holy Spirit, as evidenced by speaking in other tongues, are essential within the FGBC and Long took these concepts with him when he left the organization. All of these factors aligned with my belief system. Whenever I join a church, I think it is very important to understand its doctrine and statement of faith. If the church is directionless or has a wishy-washy, unclear doctrinal position, it may have an anything goes philosophy. In such churches, the enemy of our souls can have a field day, and the truth of the Word is not clearly defined (see: 2 Timothy 4:3; Titus 1:9). Later, when I joined the New Birth congregation, I learned that many leaders came from the Pentecostal church. If there had not been a deep Pentecostal influence at New Birth, you would not have found me in a "Baptist" church. The Holy Spirit's gifts would not be enough to make me return to a "traditional" Baptist church. Don't get me wrong; I love all of my brothers and sisters in Christ, whatever their denomination, but we all have preferences. There is a standard of holiness and sanctification that is unique to Pentecostalism. I am now used to this and would find it very difficult to sit among those who think that "speaking in tongues" and sanctification is optional (1 Peter 1:16). When God calls us to move, there is undeniable unction from the Holy Ghost, which puts a fire under us and sets us on a direct path to where God has divinely called us to go. When God says go, be obedient, and go. I've always wanted to have a spirit like Isaiah in the Bible, where He says, "Here am I send me" (Isaiah 6:8). When we say "yes" to God, His provision will follow; it is all about following His perfect plan because He is the mastermind of our destiny. The day finally came, and it was a stormy summer day in June 2007. My movers loaded the truck, and I could sense my family's disbelief. I was certainly not a baby or a very young woman. My son was seven years old, and I had only left my neighborhood once before, in 1998. Although it was time for me to go, they tried every form of emotional blackmail to persuade me to stay.

The day finally came, and everything was arranged, after much spiritual and psycho-emotional warfare. I had had long talks with my son during the previous year to prepare him as best I could. The most important thing parents can do is to consider and talk about their children's emotions and feelings during big life changes. I remembered the times when my feelings were not considered, and I felt pressured to say what my elders wanted me to say instead of what was really in my heart. Of course, parents have the final say, but we should be sensitive to our children's feelings and take them into consideration. In this case, my son was completely on board. He knew that he would lose family and friends, especially his grandmother; otherwise, he was very eager to go. I hyped him with anticipation and felt that he was ready for a new environment, both because he was enthused and also because, given his developmental stage, he probably saw this move as an adventure. The day finally came, and we were driven to the Amtrak station. My mother was nervous; her husband accompanied us to say goodbye.

We boarded the train on a cloudy, rainy day. My mother was supportive but distraught, which I could understand. However, for many months, she had verbally insulted me because I was leaving, trying to make me fearful and telling me that I would never become anything if I left her and that something was wrong with me for wanting to leave. This attitude did not improve the situation or make me want to stay, especially when she also said that I was no longer needed. My mother made it impossible for me to co-exist with her at a time when she should have been thankful for life and thankful that her daughter had earned a graduate degree. In fact, her behavior alienated me. I had read plenty of family therapy articles online about allowing family members who are very ill to verbally abuse you—and no, we don't have to take it, whatever their condition. Ultimately, she put me on the train, and I hugged her goodbye. She hugged my son goodbye, and off we went. I advised her not to worry, reminded her that her husband was with her, and told her I loved her and would see her soon.

We arrived in Georgia early the next morning with a new life on the horizon. My son's father was waiting there for us, looking happy and excited. He scooped us up with a big hug and drove us back to Gwinnett County, Georgia, to start our new lives. The house in Loganville was gone, so we moved into his apartment complex. It was very nice, and I particularly liked the landscaping. I was ready to start my life over and could not wait to get to church. At first, this was difficult, as I did not have a driver's license. Once I was settled and organized, I took some of the money I had received in the mail from the sale of my apartment and invested 1,000 dollars in Defensive Driving lessons. I learned and practiced on my own until finally, at the age of thirty-three, I had a driver's license and could use the car to drive to church or anywhere else I wanted to go. Unfortunately, I did not have enough money to do everything I needed to do. I spent four-and-a-half years in Georgia and could not find full-time employment. This felt like the strangest thing in the world. Never before, in my adult life, had I found it difficult to find a job. In Georgia, I had good luck landing interviews but never was hired. I felt there was some sort of blockage or sorcery, as if someone had consulted a witch or warlock to block my progress. Before my mother passed away, she was seeing some sort of psychic witch. I'll just leave that there. Although my experience and credentials were very good, I was never offered a full-time position.

However, Georgia did allow me to work as a substitute teacher, and I was thankful for that. I gained three extra years of experience as an educator and school counselor, becoming a certified School Counselor, which proved very helpful later on. Time passed in the state of Georgia, as it does everywhere. Every day, I prayed on my face because I had free time to linger in God's presence while my son was in school, my then-husband was at work, and I was alone with God. Initially, my son's new third-grade teacher was a disaster. A new transplant to Georgia, she was a terrible teacher who gave hardly any homework. I pulled my son out of school and homeschooled him for the rest of the year because this new school was a disaster. The school was not so bad, but the new teacher at this school created a bad situation. After homeschooling my son for the rest of the year, I decided that homeschooling was the best thing for him. He really flourished. When I opted to put him back in the school system, he tested slightly above average on his return. The bad teacher had been removed because other parents complained. My son went back to school and finished his final two years of elementary school there. I felt ready to go back to work full-time and trained and qualified as a substitute teacher. In Fall 2008, I was called in for school-system jobs on a regular basis. I finally had regular schedules at two Gwinnett County high schools and many choices and options that allowed me to work every day. I put down roots in the school community and worked as a substitute teacher for three-and-a-half years.

A few months before landing this position, I visited my mother twice. In early 2008, I learned that my mother needed to undergo radiation therapy for cancer we prayed away, which had returned in her brain. My mother underwent this ordeal while still legally married to her husband. When my mother asked me to visit, I jumped at the chance to spend time with mommy and care for her for a few weeks. I arrived in New York and, although she seemed frailer than before, I was surprised at the strength in her voice. We had talked on the phone regularly since I'd left. Eight months later, I came back to see her. Until this point, she was well enough to visit me in Georgia, and I think she would have loved seeing where I lived. She refused to come, less because of ill health than because she resented the fact that I actually left and moved to a better place. She knew that her time was short and that she would not have the opportunity to join in that life. My father, who regularly visited me in Georgia, later said that my mother would have felt good about coming to visit me because it would have eased her mind, as it did his. While I was in New York, I encountered a strange attempt to manipulate me into staying in New York, even though that was never discussed. My mother was hostile and very difficult. I cooked for her, cleaned her up, and prayed with her, but I felt very confused by the visit and the odd dynamic I was sensing. Her legal husband did not live with her, but he came over regularly, and she did not seem to want him there. However, when I arrived, she told me I wasn't needed because her husband was in charge and taking care of everything. The whole dynamic had an air of dysfunction. At the end of the visit, my mother and her husband withheld my airfare and tried to trap me into staying. My boundaries were violated, and I was nearly held against my own will, even though I had a husband and child to go home to. My mother's husband became threatening, almost as if he wanted to be physically aggressive with me. When I told my husband this on the phone, he and said, "hell no, I have the money, come home." Full of resentment, I was given a ride to the airport, and we returned home, firmly stating that we had no plans to return.

Just before I left, when my mother figured out that I was only visiting for three weeks, my mother suddenly was able to walk and get out of her wheelchair. Sadly, it appeared that she exaggerated the severity of her disability to manipulate me into leaving the life I had built in Georgia and staying in New York to take care of her. It was a very strange scenario. All I can say is that I was glad to be back in Georgia. The visit felt like an attempt to re-victimize and re-traumatize me, using the same dysfunctional dynamic that they attempted back in 1990. I said, "oh no, I have come too far spiritually, educationally, and emotionally to ever consider this kind of scenario normal." I had evolved so much as a human being that I knew they were crazy to think that it was acceptable to force me to stay under such conditions. It would not have improved my mother's overall health or been good for my child, who was with me. On my second and last visit ever to my mother in late 2008, we initially had fun, but the visit turned into a negative, volatile situation when I attempted to leave after two days. I was disciplining my son when my mother's husband once again put his hands on me as if trying to discipline me at the age of thirty-three. He yanked me from my son, threw me on the bed, and placed his hands around my throat as if he planned to choke me in front of my son. I escaped from his clutches, but my son was deeply disturbed. As usual, my mother saw everything but turned a blind eye. I hugged her goodbye, and that was the last time I ever saw her alive. When school began for my son, and I began working in the school system, sadly, my mother accused me of "abuse" to gain custody of my son before she died. Needless to say, there was no evidence of any sort. My former husband fiercely denied that I was any kind of abuser. I was abused on many levels, but I did not repeat that cycle in my own child's life; today, he would tell you that himself. When this happened, everyone knew it wasn't true, and no one could believe that my mother would stoop so low. Even my father cursed her out on the phone for trying to sabotage my life. I did not speak to my mother again until the election of Barak Obama. I was a poll worker in Gwinnett County for the 2008 Obama election, which was so exciting. I had an income from two sources, and this was a thrilling time in our history. I was still attending New Birth faithfully and praying; at that point, I had limited conversations with my mother, but after Obama was elected, we began to talk more. I could not visit her home because it was not a safe place. I refused to subject myself to negative experiences or violence during my mother's last days. Her husband convinced her that I did not care about what happened to her and persuaded my mother, under duress, to change her life insurance policy and give him her whole estate while he charged her for medical insurance.

Scriptural Nugget: 1 Corinthians 7:11, NLT

"But if she does leave him, let her remain single or else be reconciled to him. And the husband must not leave his wife."

Losing Home, Losing Her

I had a great conversation with my mother after New Year's Day in 2009. I asked whether I could spend time with her, and she thought it was very important that I did. However, when we attempted, my mother's husband said, "this is my house now," and the question of whether I could see my dying mother was "up to him, not her." I could not believe what I heard over the phone when he said this. In the end, he prevented me from saying goodbye to my mother in person. I spoke to her the evening before the morning when she passed away. That evening, she said there was so much more she had to tell me. She also said, "no fighting," and that she was so tired. I advised her over the phone to "go to sleep" if she was tired. I told her that I loved her, and that was all.

The next day, I got up and went to work at the high school. It was a cold and very sunny day. At 11 AM, I received a call from my husband, telling me that my mother's husband had informed him that my mother had left this life. I called my mother's husband to let him know that I was in class and not ignoring his call and that I was aware. We arrived in New York four days later, on the day of her wake. We drove there as quickly as we could while I struggled prayerfully for the strength to survive not only the loss of my mother but also the crazy environment. The wake was strange. My son wept in my arms while my mother's husband acted as if he wanted to snatch my child out of my arms. He intruded upon a moment when my son and I were sharing memories of my mother and his grandmother. Small, subtle things like this occurred over the two days. This man prevented me from seeing my mother's body and would not allow me to sit quietly with my mother. This scenario was appalling, traumatic, and devastating, but my mother's husband seemed to want that. He made subtle moves to intimidate me, get under people's skin, start a fight, and make a scene. None of it worked. I gave a eulogy for my mother, and others were permitted to speak. I deliberately never made a single offensive comment or negative remark, as some people may have expected. Significant people in my mother's life were missing from the service because I could not help with the funeral arrangements. This probably is because her husband did not want me in the house observing what he had done with the money my mother left for my son and me. Most of the funeral guests were his friends and family members. Only a few of the people who had meant the most to my mother before her marriage to her husband had been invited. It also looked as if he had personally excluded all of my supporters, who were key figures in her life. My father came with his wife and was supportive, but he too disliked the atmosphere. I lifted my hands in worship at the funeral when a worship song was sung, and I refused to give anyone the satisfaction of seeing me angry or hostile. After the funeral was over, I said my goodbyes, hugged my mother's former husband, thanked him graciously, and returned to Georgia. I did not stay for her internment or the reception because I had no appetite and did not want to socialize in a phony way. How could he prevent me from seeing my mother's body, place his hands around my neck, tell me I couldn't see her when she asked for me, take the money she left for me (originally from my grandmother), and then expect me to break bread with him, as if everything was ok? I was elated to go home; the three of us hopped in our vehicle and drove back to Georgia.

We arrived at 5 AM, and I never saw my mother's husband again. Shortly after, my father came to Georgia to see us for the first time. He loved it and enjoyed himself. He said that he certainly understood why I didn't plan to return to New York. A few weeks later, I received notice that my mother's husband had gone to court to claim authority over her estate. That was the final straw; I asked him what this was and why he sent it to me. After he began sending letters to my then nine-year-old son (without corresponding with me), I wrote to remind him to move on with his life. The level of disrespect he had shown to me over the years was a serious injury, and I did not want my son to think that it was acceptable to mistreat me or any other person. Although I made this clear, he persisted. I had my father call him, but he still refused to listen. Such people will violate our boundaries if we do not firmly uphold them. I had to learn to use my voice. I thought I was supposed to allow certain behaviors and take the "high road for many years." Now that I had a Master's degree in counseling and an educator's certificate, I was a new woman with an identity to uphold. I had studied human behavior and unhealthy relationships. My experiences with this man as an adolescent and an adult were more damaging than I had realized. Since we were no longer related in any way, shape, or form, he was not welcome in our lives. His persistence in contacting my son had nothing to do with love—it was about control. The enemy of our souls sometimes uses other people to disturb and destroy our peace. We must not marry people who are envious of our children from previous marriages or relationships because this can create a very volatile situation. Instead, we must carefully vet a potential partner, taking the time to get to know them. This type of familial dysfunction is very prevalent in the African-American community because Black single mothers grow tired of having to play two roles and become desperate for any male figure to enter their lives and make it all "better." For this reason, many young girls are sexually molested or violated by the next new "uncle" or so-called "father figure." This is particularly true when the mother herself has been a victim of the same cycle and has "daddy issues," as my mother did. I felt very unprotected as a teen and was then subjected to an attempted revictimization at the end of my mother's life. In life, you have to learn when to say "no more" and "enough is enough." I'm glad that I stopped living with my mother at the age of fourteen because I could have been severely damaged. I praise God for the safety of my grandmother's beautiful household. So many young women have no place to go and wind up in the arms of men— pregnant, on drugs, relying on the wrong people, and having to do crazy, damaging things just to survive. That could have been me and almost was but for the grace of God.

When I first moved to Georgia, I lived in an apartment complex that my husband had selected on his own after losing his house and facing bankruptcy. He chose it because the rent was extremely low, which made him feel safe, but I knew that we could do better. After I had a chance to explore other neighborhoods in the area, I was ready to move, but this was like pulling teeth. It is difficult for some people to go higher after a previous failure or trauma, and I was sensitive to that. I showed him that we had the financial resources to make a move and pay an extra 100 dollars for rent for a nicer, friendlier community closer to things I enjoyed in the area.

At last, he said yes. We got a great introductory deal and moved to a beautiful spot that I loved dearly. We settled there, and I decorated the place just as I had envisioned it and was very happy. We both continued to work, and my son, who was not happy in middle school, finally had a better school, where he began to thrive. I landed a long-term temporary School Counselor position at a very affluent high school in Gwinnett County. This job allowed me to gain more experience and discover what I liked and did not like professionally. High School Counseling is a very administrative, paperwork-oriented, and data-directed job, which does not involve much counseling. For this reason, I felt very disappointed with my role.

In 2010, Bishop Eddie Long was accused of involvement in a "sex scandal" with some young men at the church. I was there when he declared he had "five stones to fight with" but did not definitively deny the charges. I stood by Bishop Long at an emotional level, but it was difficult to watch the crowds dwindle at New Birth. It was hurtful to see the phony congregation up and abandon their pastor. Colleagues at the high school said that it wasn't good for their careers (as educators) to attend a church where there was a scandal involving minors. I knew they were right—it did not look good professionally. Although I continued to be a part of New Birth, I gradually began to watch the services online and visit the Ausar Auset Society Atlanta to supplement my spirituality. I read all of the Metu Neter books and studied them well; they transformed my life. I was not disillusioned with the church or spiritually weakened by the alleged situation at New Birth, but I needed to figure out where I belonged. I could tell that a life shift was forthcoming. Anyone who has a solid foundation in the Bible can see that the Metu Neter books amplify the main three monotheistic religions' principles. The Ausar Auset Society is a monotheistic, Kemetic, and spirituality-based organization that teaches its initiates how to adjust their behavior, bodies, spirit, and psychological thought patterns when facing life's challenges. I am thankful to have come across it. Some people who are very "religious" misinterpret it as a pagan system that involves worshipping other "gods" and doing witchcraft and sorcery; this could not be further from the truth, especially in the way I applied it. I will not discuss the Ausarian spiritual system's details in this book, although I may discuss it in future writings, God willing. Organizations like Asaur Auset and other African spiritual systems usually do not proselytize, evangelize, attempt to convert or lure people from their current spiritual paths. A person of any faith can apply these principles while retaining their original religious beliefs. However, some in the Christian community thought that simply because I practiced meditation and applied some psychological principles of Ausar Auset that do not contradict the Bible, I was lost, evil, and likely to taint the local Christian body with these teachings. FALSE! If I am in a Christian setting and expected to teach Bible-based principles, then that is what I am going to do. I am not saying that Christians should practice or mix Christianity with other faiths, and I do not proselytize for the Ausar Auset Society as a spiritual system.

I studied the organization's books for psychological and personal enrichment, just as one would go to an Iyanla Vanzant conference, purchase her books, or watch her TV show, given that she belongs to the Yoruba/New Thought faith. The visualization strategies I learned from those books and seminars helped me transition to the next chapter in my life, with God Almighty's help. Time passed, and I felt miserable. I still couldn't find a full-time position in Georgia. Although I was gaining years of experience in the field of education, my financial situation was troubling. I was in a good place in some ways: my credit score was 700, and I could see the mighty hand of God providing for me, but why should I have to seek provision or beg my husband for basic things? At times, my husband was verbally abusive, using anger and outbursts to manipulate situations, blame me for the verbal abuse, and yell. To gain leverage, he would often withhold funds from me, making it difficult for me to visit places and get around. When I look back on where I was then and where I am now, I realize how isolated I was in Georgia. I got to see and explore some nice things, but my limited resources made it difficult to enjoy traveling locally and exploring. Had I enjoyed my current circumstances in Georgia, things would have been very different. At one point, my husband and I considered buying a house. I felt our credit rating was right; my husband's bankruptcy and foreclosure had passed the allotted time frame so that he was able to purchase another home. We chose a gorgeous home in Gwinnett county and were about to close the deal with an excellent mortgage when, at the last minute, my husband chickened out and blocked the sale by refusing to close. I was embarrassed and devastated. We had a great salesman who was honest and tried to get us the best possible mortgage rate through an FHA loan. I felt that my former husband had strung me along and played with my emotions. When he backed out of the deal, I was livid. A few months later, my husband lost the wonderful job he had had for six years. Perhaps he knew that something was happening and did not disclose it to me. Disconnection was the theme of our marriage: no conversation and limited communication. He had a wife who was open-minded and could talk about a wide variety of topics, but all he ever wanted to do was to come home at the end of the day and watch TV. He preferred watching DVDs of 1980s cartoons to talking with me.

As time went on, the separation and loneliness were killing me. I was bored and tired of being mistreated. I also needed a change. I begged God to free me from the marriage, both financially and emotionally. I really grew to dislike my husband. I became angry at myself and frustrated with being locked into a marriage that made me miserable. I did have joy in my life, but I was worried about my career and wondered when a breakthrough would ever occur. I grew so agitated that it was truly time to move and go to Florida after much prayer and consultation. When you are ready to go, God will agitate you to the point of discontent; you will become dissatisfied with your situation. God truly created a way for me to escape. However, sometimes when He creates an escape route, we do not seize the opportunity. It takes faith and God's timing to branch out and break free from relationships and situations that have kept us bound for a long time. So, full of faith, we packed up and moved to South Florida. My husband got a job in Florida doing cable, and I had potential interviews on the table, but still no guarantees, just a pocket full of faith. I was very sick with the flu, which I rarely catch, but the stress was suppressing my immune system; I was also trying to pack up a house alone, with a twelve-year-old in tow. Finally, after setting up shop for a few weeks and staying with a relative in South Florida, my husband returned to Georgia and helped us pack our things. Then we drove to Florida. I was emotional about leaving Georgia because so much growth had taken place in my life. Before leaving, I had made some good professional connections; I worked a part-time job for extra money, doing computer survey work. I truly enjoyed that position, and I needed the money. So, after packing up, we got on the road and drove to Fort Lauderdale. I was very, very happy. I knew that everything would work out eventually, and it did.

We made it to our new apartment in Florida, which was nothing compared to our home in Georgia. I knew that our new place was temporary. As before, my husband had worked things out while "I directed him." I had selected everything via the Internet. As I could not get there physically to see things for myself, I trusted his judgment. The place was livable, but not what we were used to. I had a job interview the day after I arrived in Florida but did not hear anything from that company for several weeks. In a week and a half, I had landed a job in a call center that I applied for as a brief backup plan because my husband's hours had been reduced, and I needed to rescue us by contributing to the rent. However, while working at this decent low-wage job, which I was very over-qualified for, I got a response to my initial interview for the job I actually wanted and was hired with real pay! I was overjoyed, went through training, and then got another call two weeks later from the online university I had prayed about for so many years! I nailed my interview and finally had a breakthrough, landing my first full-time job as an Academic Advisor! It took sooooooooo long! I prayed sooooooo hard for soooo many years! Despite the great recession and after shedding many tears and thinking that there was something wrong with me or I didn't have enough experience, I got the job. I resigned from the other place, completed four weeks of training, and joined my team on the floor, in and out of the conference/classroom. My goodness, that job was challenging, tedious, and tiring. It came with great money and benefits, but three months later, the man who hired me was fired. Then there were major cuts and department downsizing. The university became a very scary place to work. It was terrifying to arrive for work and hear that 700 people were laid off campus-wide and at various regions. After that, there was restructuring: people with fewer qualifications were labeled advisors. Titles were changed from Academic Advisors to Education Advisors. It just became a mess. We got a new campus president and a new advising director; initially, both seemed supportive, but they were not. I learned never to discuss my academic/career goals with people above me, who fear being replaced. They will come for you and make things uncomfortable. Eventually, I had to leave because the environment became too scary and toxic. I am glad that I did because, a few years later, the company was bought out by another institution and ceased to exist. After Kaplan University, I worked for a smaller, independently owned career college as a student-support specialist, which allowed me to continue in my career field on a smaller scale with less pay. I loved that position. I was treated much better than I had been at my previous place of employment. The environment was stress-free and lots of fun. Life was finally calm, but I did not have my previous benefits or pay, so we had to re-budget. God still provided for our family and favored us.

My father had made his first visit to Florida the year before that while I was working at Kaplan. I arranged for him to meet us in Orlando and bought a Disney World ticket and hotel room for about five days for the four of us. We had a wonderful time. It was the experience of a lifetime that my father and I never got to share when I was a child. I felt so good being able to give my father such a special trip because he told me that he had never had a vacation to a distant place since he was with my mother. He mentioned that my taste in hotels was similar to hers. I said, "Well, she introduced me to quality places to stay, so I am going to go for what I know." We spent a day with my in-laws and had dinner at my husband's father's house. My father really enjoyed himself and felt very welcomed. On the last day of our visit, I could see my father's face as we sat in the dining area outside the Earl of Sandwich to enjoy the sun and scenery. He took in everything one last time before he left. He was thrilled, and it was a joy to share that with him, just as I could share other great moments with him, which I will always treasure. During the Disney trip, I still had my old car. We drove from south Florida to Orlando. That car was on its last leg, and the battery died during our trip. I realized that it was time for me to get a new car of my own. In 2013, I did just that. I began to post pictures of my life on social media and gained a huge following. I was interviewed in various online forums and live streams. People asked me to do their online shows and speak at other people's events I co-hosted New York Local activist Tony Nix's talk show,

"Enough is Enough, Save Our Children." This opportunity was wonderful for me, as I developed great connections on social media, which I still have. Everywhere, people were direct-messaging me, asking me to mentor and counsel them, and making other similar requests. I did not ask for any of this—it just happened. Prominent figures in the conscious community, community activists, and old-school R&B celebrities commented on my page. Some asked to mentor me and invited me to work with them. I did not realize that my light was shining in a way that would draw lots of artificial love and lots of hate. My husband hated and despised my online popularity. I believe that people who followed me online saw me as greater than I saw myself. I should have gotten more protection, such as a mentor, assistant, or manager.

In terms of my marriage, this was an extremely dark time in my life. I was being ignored, and there was no conversation. Even when I tried to engage in a positive and loving conversation, I got the brush off. I tried to create a happy life for our family: my job was paying for my husband's two-year degree, and I had him on my health insurance, along with my son, until he got his own. I was carrying a lot, and he was making good money, but what is prosperity in a marriage when there is no love, conversation, friendship, peace, or joy. I believe that my husband was jealous because I finally had an excellent professional position. Life was better for him when I had little to no money and depended on him for most things. That is not the way to live in marriage; we must live in truth and authenticity. On social media, I made a marriage relationship request so that the public could see us both. He refused to allow that status to be public on his page. He wanted the world to think he was single so that he could talk to women on Facebook. Nevertheless, I was all about my family on Facebook and proud of what I was doing in my life.

Scriptural Nugget: John 4:24 NLT
"For God is Spirit, so those who worship him must worship in spirit and in truth."

Slander and Betrayal

I began to rebel and find attention elsewhere. I began an emotional affair with a man online who gave me the attention I craved. However, this attention also created enemies. The individual was in the limelight and had a lot to lose professionally and personally if any information was released. One or two women were affiliated with this person, and they were very envious of his interest in me; I, therefore, became a target. The person would salute me on Facebook and post my picture on his page for his followers and fans. These actions made people think that we had a deeper connection than we actually did. Given my spiritual convictions and signs from the Lord about this friendship's improper nature and direction, I abruptly blocked and removed the person I was talking to. Now, the devil was angry with me; right afterward, all hell broke loose. My theory is that folks thought I would blow the whistle on them, using sensitive information, because they had large followings, and therefore decided to get *me* before I got *them*. Of course, this was ridiculous. I planned to go quietly and never mention a thing. Blocking someone does not always signify hostility; sometimes, people just don't want to be connected anymore, as in my case.

I was totally unprepared for the conspiracy that unfolded, which I could have prevented by staying on the right side of things. However, I guess I became complacent and let my guard down on too many levels. I confused artificial cyber love for real love and loyalty because I could not get what I needed from home or seek a deeper love from the Lord, which only He can give. However, I do not mean to imply that we can or should allow ourselves to be neglected by those we are in covenant with. As a result of all of the hype online, several people watched and observed me. They were obsessed with my life and accomplishments and who I was talking to and obviously wanted to see me go down. Awful and ridiculous rumors began to circulate. Although nobody could tell me exactly what was being said, there were innuendos. I was able to piece together the rumors and identify the culprit. My page had apparently been hacked to make it look as if I had posted something damming, which was quickly erased by those who wanted to harm me. There were supposedly also photo-shopped images that placed me in compromising scenes or situations. I have never seen these pictures, and no one has ever been brave enough to tell me what they were. However, people who saw these fabrications felt confident that I needed some "help" and needed to "love myself " (I'm still laughing hysterically). My Facebook feed began to turn on me, accusing me of sinister acts that I knew nothing about. They accused me of twisted perversions and all kinds of sexual deviance. Their accusations were too ridiculous and outrageous for me to comment on, reply to, or defend. I was shocked and then traumatized as so-called Facebook friends began to disappear slowly, each one saying something derogatory about me.

I knew that something was terribly wrong, and worst of all, it carried over into my professional life. The person contacted my employer via social media because my place of employment was listed on my social media profile. The aim was to make my work life crazy so that my employers would no longer respect me. I had posted positive pictures of work, and the social-media predators hated that too. Someone concocted the story that I had confided in them about a "past life." Such efforts were designed to make me seem phony to all my followers. I could not believe that this was happening. After everything I had poured into my followers every day, supporting them both spiritually and educationally, someone was gloating over my destruction and said that I needed to take responsibility for the destruction *they* were causing. I downloaded and deleted my page and launched a fresh one. This whole scenario was frightening and disheartening. I had made a prior donation online; a few weeks later, my bank account was hacked because the donation and business transactions were connected to the social-media predators. I was able to track where my bank account was hacked from and later traced the hack to the region where the social-media predators did business. I reported this incident to the police and planned to take legal action, but the Holy Spirit sat heavily on me. For a time, I could not speak, write, or defend myself publicly. I later hired an investigator to monitor the suspects online. Out of fear, I again briefly befriended the person I had cut off, hoping things would calm down. When they did, I parted ways with that individual as peacefully as I could. They still sent spies to my page to befriend me. While I was slanderously attacked, the gift of tongues began to bubble up inside me almost as powerfully as it had when I had first received it. It felt as if the Holy Spirit put a muzzle on my mouth and gave me a peace that passed all understanding. I will sadly disclose that my husband seemed almost happy that these things were happening to me. He was jealous of all the positive attention I received online from numerous people and the positive opportunities that came my way as a result.

    I contributed so much to many people online through my positive words, posts, and videos, even before Facebook Live became popular. Then, all of a sudden, none of that counted or mattered. After years of sitting under all of that "good" word in church, being delivered, "working out my soul's salvation with fear and trembling" according to (Philippians 2:12). After being filled with the Holy spirit, dedicating my life to in-depth study, becoming a professional Black woman. And becoming an activist, teaching Black history online, celebrating womanhood, and dropping jewels given to me by the Spirit of God, suddenly, I became a person created in someone else's imagination. Feeling paranoid, I wondered whether the conspiracy had been even larger than I imagined. I felt that the accusations, murmuring, and chattering also insulted my mother and grandmother's legacy. My mother and grandmother raised me to be a "lady," well-spoken and classy, with self-respect. My mother was Black and proud, my father was a class act, and my grandmother was certainly a class act. Slandering me was attempting to dismantle everything they invested in me. I would never live a lifestyle that would displease them, my son, or my God, causing shame or disgrace. Have I always done everything right? No. Have I made the wrong choices? Absolutely! Have I always been wise and upright every waking moment? No. But I would never adopt a habitually degrading lifestyle—absolutely NEVER. For one thing, I am too much of a germaphobe and hypochondriac to do such things. I carry state certification that allows me to work with young people, and I am neither professionally suicidal nor self-destructive. Besides, my ex-husband is not a weak or foolish man who would allow himself to be played. The rumors and lies were insulting to his manhood; nor would I marry a foundationally weak man, given how strong I am. I am still waiting for a public confession from this person so that we can have an open live-forum discussion about this so-called "past life" that they created. However, the person has yet to come forward to discuss the story they circulated openly. I come from a line of fiercely independent women who were very feisty and strong. My mother told me what her mother had told her and, to this day, I can't be bought. She said, "never take money or expensive gifts from a man who is not your husband or father. Never give a man who is not your husband the key to your door. He will think he owns you and may try to gain leverage over you." The bottom line, as the Psalm (101:5) says, "Whoever slanders their neighbor in secret, I will put to silence."

According to Proverbs 19:5, "A false witness will not go unpunished, nor will a liar escape." The suspect(s) are presently not doing well; I pray for God's mercy on their lives and hope that they will confess, repent, and give their lives to Christ Jesus. Less than a year later, God prepared a table in the presence of my enemies with abundant blessings, as the upcoming pages will show (Psalm 23:5). For this reason, it was so important to hold my peace and let God fight my battles (Exodus 14:14). Fast forward to the brighter side of life: I had applied for a new job and did not hear anything for a few weeks. During this time, my father came down for a visit, and we had a good time going to the movies, the malls, a restaurant, and the beach. However, there was spoken and unspoken drama that I would not have brought to him had I known what was about to happen. During his visits with me in Florida, my father said, "I promised your mother I would live," and "how much more can you take, Lori?" I did not understand what he was saying until much later, when it all made sense. My father was preparing me for what was to come so that I would be mentally and psychologically ready. God bless his soul; he was trying to protect me from the inevitable. I finally heard back from the job I had applied for. As I had begun a doctoral program in Pastoral Counseling in 2013, I decided to apply for a job at the same institution. My school was the online version, and the job applied for was at the brick and mortar version in the Tampa region, northwest of where we lived in southeast Florida. I had the divine itch to move because the rent was getting too high, even though our place was fabulous and wonderful. The Holy Spirit said it was time to go. This transition was sudden, but I knew it was a God move because I sought god, prayed, and received confirmation. I was in the middle of a crazy situation at my former job, where the slander had caused chaos. It was like God snatched me up and miraculously relocated me, with a 10,000 dollar salary increase. I rejoiced when I got the news, gave my two weeks' notice, and quickly researched the region to find a place that resembled our home in South Florida to create continuity for my son. My husband had to quickly find a new job, and he struggled with this, but I believed God. When the leasing office where we were moving from tried to charge us 3,000 dollars to leave, I called an attorney to handle this unfair charge, which was quickly reduced to less than 600 dollars; amen! We put our possessions in storage because we could not afford to move them at a moment's notice. I waited until we were paid and then took the money and paid for a moving truck.

We spent about three weeks sleeping on the floor of our new place, which was unfurnished. That was a first for me, but the sacrifice was worth it—and we got our things a few weeks later. I remember when we first arrived at the new place; it was a duplex in a very exclusive suburban apartment complex that God told me would be the right place for us when I saw it for the first time. My son was almost fourteen and so adorable. He said, "Mom, this is our new place?" He was very upset about leaving his friends and our paradise-like place in South Florida. Until he saw the new apartment, he did not want to relocate. However, when we arrived, he exclaimed, "Ma, this is like MTV Cribs!" I thought that was really funny, and after all the tears he cried as we drove, it told me that my son was pleased with being suddenly whisked away to yet another location. When we finally got settled, my husband could not find a job like the one he had had in South Florida, making him angry and upset. When I began my new job, I also knew that it was not where I needed to be. Four weeks after I started, the campus president left, and people started slowly disappearing. Major administrators were let go, including the boss who had hired me. I had no leadership, no training, and no help in an institution that was anti-African-American. I expressed my disappointment to my father, who was surprised but wanted me to find a position where I could become professionally stable. Unusually, he also said that he wanted to see his grandson on his birthday. To do this, I would have to pay for my father's plane ticket again when we were just getting back on our feet. We still owed some money in South Florida, my husband was unemployed, and the house was not fully set up. I then caught a bad case of the flu and was under the weather.

Looking back, I really wish my father had told us the truth, as I would have bent over backward to make it a reality for him to hang out with his grandson. The last time I was with my father, we spent quality time together, and he shared positive aspects of his health situation with me. Although he seemed to be in excruciating pain, when I questioned him, he brushed it off. I asked again what was wrong with him, and he dismissed the question, even though he grunted every time he sat down. All in all, we had a great time. I remember buying patio furniture just for him so that we could gaze out at the tropical sunset on my patio, which overlooked the water. It was truly beautiful. God spoke to me clearly, saying: on the last night, have your father look out at this beautiful sight and share this with him. I am so glad that I did and that I was able to cook for him and provide him with luxury and rest while he was with me. I am also thankful that his wife allowed him to come and spend that time with me. She knew that such times were important. During his whole visit with me, he lived clean and never had a drink. I took him to the airport and spent time with him, and oddly, he held me like a baby, as if I were five years old. I thought this was endearing and comforting but odd because his hugs were usually very firm, loving, and strong.

I hugged and kissed him and went out to the parking lot to find my car; at that moment, I suddenly became disoriented and confused. The sun was beaming down hot, as it always does in South Florida, but I was gripped with anxiety; although I *do not have* anxiety attacks, I could feel the parking lot getting larger. I couldn't find my car, and I wanted to run back inside the airport to be with my father, but it was too late. I wandered in circles around the lot, going upstairs and downstairs. For about 35 minutes, I could not find my car. Then, just as I was about to call for help, I finally located it. Little did I know that that day would be the last time I spent with my father in this life, which I believe is why I had that strange and disorienting experience.

Fast-forwarding back to our new life in New Tampa, I continued to work, but my husband couldn't find a job and became more hostile. His hostility was already a brewing problem. I always used to think that things would get better and our problems would go away as soon as we had a better environment, a bigger space, or a new house. However, none of these things can change a naturally unhappy person. I always used to tell him that only God could fill those empty spaces, replacing anger with His peace and joy. I knew that, as his wife, I was not enough. No one could ever be enough because only God can fix, repair, restore, and heal us where we have been damaged and hurt. As Jesus said in (John 4:14), "Whoever drinks of the water that I will give him will never thirst again." If a person is unwilling to drink, however, there is nothing anyone can do. The holidays were approaching, and I was carrying my family. My husband slept on the couch, as we had limited furniture. My son had furniture, and I bought a bed of my own. I refused to sleep with my husband because his mistreatment of me had escalated. It bothered him that I was the breadwinner and temporary sole provider, and he took his anger out on me. He had to sell his truck because it broke down, and he took out a loan to support the family and buy a new vehicle. I prayed for him since he was often curled up in a ball on the floor or lying on the couch watching TV in a state of depression instead of using the tools he had previously acquire to combat his depression, fear, anger, and anxiety about the current situation. I became the positive one and bought my husband an aventurine stone that I prayed over for prosperity, along with a tiger's eye stone and some jade. Some people might call this witchcraft, but these stones could be perceived similarly to the anointed prayer cloths that you can buy from preachers on TV. They represented a point of contact for my faith. On its own, the stone has no power. To trust in the power of rocks, instead of trusting THE ROCK, which is Christ Jesus, would be idolatrous indeed (1 Corinthians 10:4): "And did all drink the same spiritual drink: for they drank of that spiritual Rock that followed them: and that Rock was Christ."

In the Bible, we read of stones being used for Godly purposes, albeit not for healing or anything deemed "New Age." The high priest in the Old Testament, for example, wore a breastplate featuring twelve stones. According to (Exodus 28:17-21), these stones—sardius, topaz, emerald, turquoise, sapphire, diamond, jacinth, agate, amethyst, beryl, onyx, and jasper—represent the twelve tribes of Israel, just as every time the priest ministers, he represents all the people to God. Revelation 21 includes another list of precious stones, all of them in New Jerusalem. These stones were set in the foundations of the wall to beautify this city.

"Each and every stone was created by God for Him" (Colossians 1:16). "These stones, even the plain ones we see lying on the roadside, give praise and glory to God" (Luke 19:40). "As such, they are for God alone." Source:(Christianity Today, JB Cachila, 2017).

I am not promoting the use of crystals as a healing and protection source or telling the reader that they have superpowers. WE may hold a stone or crystal close to our heart while we are praying to THE CREATOR who CREATED it, knowing the intention of our prayer and praying in that direction. If I know that I need a financial blessing, I may hold a piece of jade (which is said to represent finances and prosperity) while praying to my heavenly Father. The stone simply helps to keep my mind focused on what I am praying about with a specific intention. Is this a requirement or recommended way of making prayers more powerful or likely to be heard? NO! It is simply a personal preference. As (Romans 1:25) says, "They traded the truth about God for a lie. So they worshiped and served the things God created instead of the Creator himself, who is worthy of eternal praise! Amen." It is important to stress that I do not practice witchcraft, astral travel, psychic phenomena, or idolatry. Equally, I do not worship or give reverence to any source other than the Creator of the Universe. According to (1 Peter 2:4), "And coming to Him as to a living _stone_ which has been rejected by men, but is choice and precious in the sight of God." Yeshua, aka Jesus, is the rock of our salvation, and yes, we can go to the rock, which is higher than ourselves.

Thanksgiving came. Although I usually spent the holiday with my in-laws, that year, I was very dejected, hurt, and angry about my husband's indifference and hostility toward me at a time when I was trying to pump him up. The fact that I was making progress in my life made him hold me in contempt. Finally, he was offered a telephone company position while he was working a temporary job to help pay the bills. He took the test, passed, and was hired, with training beginning four weeks from that date. Things were looking up, and my prayers had been heard. However, my job was not comfortable or happy; unfortunately, it still wasn't a good fit. With no proper training, I felt that I was being set up to fail. Thank goodness I did not depend on this job for free tuition, as people always assumed I did.

Around that time, my spirit had been leading me to pray for Bishop Eddie L. Long. However, I did not know why I felt that I had to speak with him face to face. God told me to pray for him, and so I drove all the way to Georgia and stayed with a friend for the 2015 New Year's Eve celebration. When I arrived, I could see that the service was no longer packed full of people, although he was still holding two services. I went to the first service, which was wonderful; I was glad to be in the house of God. Yes, I did pray for Bishop Eddie L. Long from my seat, as the Holy Spirit did not free me up to make physical contact after the service, but I wish that I had. I had planned to get a picture with him, but I felt the need to leave after the service, without lingering. I felt sad to leave. Before the service that night, I had been crying and praying in my car outside Whole Foods in John's Creek, longing to return to Georgia. My phone rang, and it was my father. He listened as I talked, and I wiped away the tears upon hearing his voice. He told me that he wanted me to be happy wherever I was and that I would do well anywhere. He wanted me to be rooted and planted somewhere so that I could thrive. My father shared his hopes and prayers for me toward the end of 2014. He affirmed and confirmed that I did not need to reconnect with anyone from the past who was left behind in Co-op City (specifically, my mother's last husband). My father and I were in agreement with closing the door to our past in the Bronx, NY. He also said that he hoped that I would find a good "Baptist" church with good people in it. I chastised him over the phone, saying, "Daddy, I'm Pentecostal, not Baptist." He had gone to new Birth with me and seen Eddie Long live and was highly impressed with New Birth. I remember the intensity of our conversation on the phone while I was in the car outside Whole Foods, where I had taken him during previous visits. He did not mention wanting to visit the place where I was, as he normally did when we talked, and I thought that was odd. When my son and I returned home from Georgia, my father phoned from New York to tell me that he had "a bit of malignancy in the colon" after having some tests done the previous month. I told him that as soon as he came out of the hospital, we would radically change his diet. Strangely, he did not respond, although he would normally say something to the effect of "Yeah, we can try that." But during my phone conversation with him in the car in Georgia, his response suggested that he did not see a future to work toward. About thirty days before this conversation, the Lord had called me to a heavy time of prayer and consecration. The Holy Spirit advised me to pray without ceasing for thirty days in the month of November 2014. Before this, I had been praying fervently about our move, which was prompted by slander and harassment. At the time, I did not understand why I was called to pray, but I am so glad I listened because I became highly sensitive. My hearing was very fine-tuned to the voice of the Lord.

My father went into the hospital and told me how to contact his doctors and the time of his surgery. After a few days, I told my son, who spoke to his grandfather on the phone. My father said, "This will not be like your grandmother," and eerily, he was right. Strangely, it was far worse. I was at work, and I had not heard a word from my father's wife. All was silent, even though he had gone into surgery the previous night. When I phoned her, she said that my father was in ICU. Her statement did not register with me because she said it so calmly. She did not say, "Lori, you'd better get to New York," because my father had told her not to. I do not blame her, as she was being his "ride or die." However, I did have a right to know how serious his condition was. I had not processed how something my father described as "minor" could be progressing so fast. His wife did tell me, however, that my father was pissed off when he woke up. Otherwise, she did not elaborate. Supposedly, there was some delay. I believe that when he woke up, he had gotten the devastating news that his condition was far worse than he imagined. A day or so later, I was able to speak with my father, who sounded great. We talked about how he was eager to go home to recover. My father sounded quite optimistic, as I was also. The next day, when I talked to him, he complained that he was indeed hungry and could not keep any food down. For that reason, they could not let him go home. Sadly, he never did.

My father grew weaker and could only speak to me for short intervals. When I spoke to him for the last time, he sounded like a ninety-year-old man. No one phoned to tell me to come to New York ASAP; even while he was dying, my father pretended to be healthier than he was in order to protect me. He told me, for example, that he was looking forward to getting out of the hospital. We had our last conversation while I was going to Taco Bell to get a bean burrito. When I got home, I said to my son, "I don't like the way your grandfather sounded at all; he sounded like he was ninety years old." Two hours later, the hospital phoned to warn me that my father was failing. He had choked on his stomach contents because he could not keep anything down. What was happening to him caused him to go into cardiac arrest due to atrial fibrillation. They said that he was unconscious and that they would call me back. Earlier that night, my social media post included a prophetic utterance: "The Lord giveth and the Lord taketh away, blessed be the name of the Lord," which is a quote from (Job 1:21). I guess the Holy Spirit was preparing me for what was to come. I immediately knew that I had to STOP, DROP, and PRAY. I fell to the floor on my face and began brutally interceding for my father, weeping and pleading. Then I changed positions and began to walk my bedroom floor in the dark, praying in English and also in tongues. I believe that my father was briefly revived during this time, but I could not lay hands on him because I was not in the room. The Physician's Assistant called me and said: "Your father is leaving this life. He came up for a minute, and he's a fighter, Lori. Is there anything you want me to tell him?" I wept and said, yes, "that I love him very much." They called me back and said they were sorry, but my father was gone. They had told him what I said, and he loved me too. I walked out of my bedroom, which had become the war room, and I told my son that his grandfather was gone. Then I told my husband. They could not believe it. My son shut the door and cried. My husband didn't hold me—he apologized and went into the bathroom to weep because he really liked my father. Then I began to process everything. After an hour or so, my blood began to boil. EVERYTHING that had happened over the last nine years started to make sense. I remembered statements that my father had made, such as: "I just wanna live" and "I promised your mother that I would live." My parents had a private face-to-face talk after my mother came out of the hospital following her brain surgery. They had kicked me out of the house for an hour. I was not privy to what they shared, but the Holy Spirit later revealed to me that they had discussed both of their prognoses and opted not to tell me that they both had cancer at the same time because it would be too much for me. I was in graduate school at the time, and they wanted to spare me so that I would succeed. I thank God for their protective covenant, which kept me from worrying. However, they did not know how spiritually strong I was. My mother used to say, "I hope you and your stepfather can get along…you're going to need each other one day." Well, I have grown in this life and learned that we do not need to be attached to things or people that repeatedly hurt us, even for the sake of peace or forgiveness.

During the last few months of his life, my father told me over the phone that he totally understood why I left New York. He said it was the right thing for me to do and that there was no need to re-connect with my mother's husband. So, my father gave me my marching orders toward the end. He also thanked me in that same conversation for all the trips, vacations, and time we had spent together, which was eerie. He thanked me for showing him "the other side of life." It is now obvious that this was my cue. I said to him, "you don't have to thank me," not realizing that this was his way of saying goodbye. I did not (or perhaps could not) process his words. Fast forward to January 2015—I am a month away from my 40th birthday, and my father is gone; I must pull myself together. After realizing that he was sicker than I ever knew, I became angry. I remembered one time when he had wanted to come to Georgia. As neither of us had any money, I advised him to get a plane in New York City instead of upstate New York, where he lived. My "stepsister" criticized me for that, saying, "he can't make that kind of journey because he's too sick." I said, "what do you mean? I know he has knee issues because he told me that he'd had a knee replacement due to deteriorating cartilage.

This report was not true; his problem was far worse. At the time, I had not understood why my stepsister was so upset. Now it all made sense. I was glad that I'd been able to take my father to Disney World and show him new environmental beauty every time he came to see me. My father's wife phoned me almost two hours after he had lost his battle. She said, "Lori, your father is gone." I said, "I know, the doctors told me. But I need you to tell me the truth. What stage was his cancer? He was much sicker than we knew." She said that cancer had spread to his lymph nodes, although the doctors may not have known until he was in the hospital.

Although I still felt that she was evasive, I let it go because I could hear my father spiritually saying: "Lori, I need you to go to my wife." Shortly after, my father's brother called to say that my father's wife had just phoned him: "Lori, this is crazy, he said. He had to be sicker than we ever knew." He shared my feelings and felt angry with my father for hiding his condition from us. My uncle pointed out how ironic it was that my father's passing was uncannily similar to that of his mother, who went into the hospital for surgery, which was "botched." When a person is in relatively good health before going into the hospital but never recovers and winds up **dead** (a word I do not like to use), the family's first impulse is to sue someone. However, I did not think about this until later. It was time to go to New York. But how? This loss was all so sudden. As I did not know what was coming, I hadn't stashed any money to fly myself and the family to New York. I had no choice but to rent a car and drive to New York with my then fourteen-year-old son. My husband had to start training for the new job that he had waited for, for so long during his period of depression. He asked whether he could postpone or skip the training to go to my father's funeral but was told that he would have to start three months from the original date. We needed that additional salary, so I told my husband to do the training. I knew that my father was happy about his job and would have wanted him to go to training. I could almost hear my father saying that within me: that he wanted my husband to start his job. I had my son, God, and myself, and we would be fine. I called the car rental company, and I called my job in tears, explaining why I had to leave. Thankfully, my mother's "sister-friend," whom I had known since I was a baby, who lived in Maryland, allowed me to use her home as a rest stop between

Maryland and New York so that I could rest and break the trip in half after driving from Florida. The car rental company said that I would have to wait four hours for a same-day car. My husband provided travel cash, and my son and I were able to go. When we arrived at the car rental place, the man who got the car for us was named Nick, which was my father's first name. These incidences helped me see that my father was still rocking with me and made it to the hereafter. My father was Nicholas, and my mother was Saundra; the car we picked up was a white Nissan. White is the color historically worn by the family members of someone who has passed. After I had completed the paperwork for the car, which seemed to take an eternity, the driver brought me to the rental place to collect the car. Off we went at almost 4 PM; the sun was starting to set. As I started up the navigator and plugged in the address, I knew that it would be a very, very, very long drive. My son and I were setting out on a two-day road trip to New York. The road was long, and my phone constantly rang as family members and friends checked in to make sure that we were OK on the road. I had not slept the night before and was very tired. I pushed up through I 75 until I could transition to the I 95 corridor, where I found myself in an unfamiliar part of Georgia, heading towards Savannah. I arrived in Savannah, somewhat confused. It began to get cold, but I was dressed for the cold. I stopped for gas and food, drove north, and pulled over for a quick nap at a Georgia rest stop.

A week before my father's passing, I learned that I had a mysterious lump in my breast. I never told my father about this lump, as it was the last thing he needed to hear. As my doctor was looking for suspicious signs, and my father had passed away, I asked God, "What have I done? Lord, this is not the God I know because you would not put more on me than I can bear. God, you are a good Father. You would not allow the enemy to pull a double or triple whammy like this on our family, nor would you do this to such a good child as my son. So I drove to New York with a painful lump in my right breast, which the stress of the event seemed to make more painful. I unfastened my bra to stop myself from thinking about the pain. As I drove, other parts of my body also began to hurt. I had neck pain, breast pain, and slight congestion; as the waves of tears fell, I called out to God, prayed, and talked to my son for strength. That drive was one of the hardest things I had ever had to do in my life, but I could hear my father's voice internally, telling me when to pull over. In the Spirit world, he seemed deeply apologetic. I had a dream about my father immediately after he had transitioned; we had an intense conversation, although I cannot recall what he told me. I just knew that he was very disturbed about how things happened and that his leaving was not his plan but God's. I felt suspicious and questioned whether my enemies could have murdered him. The devil played all kinds of tricks to prevent me from focusing on my entire family's healing. I believe that my father was hit by a spiritual attack linked to the warfare that I was facing through slander and harassment. I was engaged in heavy warfare prayers, and I honestly believe that my father (in a spiritual sense) took a bullet that was meant for me. I believe that he knew and understood what I was going through. Had I understood his situation, I wouldn't have talked about my troubles as much and would've concentrated more on what was happening to him.

While driving to New York, I remembered that my assignment was to reach his wife, as he had asked after his passing. His main concern was that I reach everyone in NY. Before leaving, I had called his siblings. His two sisters were sad but detached. I did not push them any further. Instead, I reached out to my Uncle, who called me regularly during my travels. At last, I made it to South Carolina and found myself driving on Orangeburg's outskirts, where my father's family came from. I could feel him telling me to stop at the rest stop there, where I would be safe because the ancestors (my angels) will be watching over me. I trusted this instruction and began to swerve. When a cop pulled me over, I explained our journey and stepped out of the car with my son. The officer was concerned because he had seen me swerving. After I explained that I was bereaved and driving from Florida to New York for my father's funeral, who had died suddenly the previous evening, he understood and suggested I find the nearest rest stop. He also offered his condolences. So, I found a rest stop not too far away and took a nap. At dawn, I persevered. I knew that I would be safe in South Carolina and I felt divinely guided there. However, I was also very sad, knowing that I had no connection to my family in the region and could not knock on anyone's door to say, "Can I stay the night? I just lost my dad." In truth, I am fairly sure that they would have opened their doors to me, but that's neither here nor there. I continued driving, had something to eat, fed my son, and called my friends and family. Friends were also phoning me, and I kept them advised of my whereabouts. I was determined to reach the North Carolina, Virginia area. I pressed on, wishing that my son was old enough to take the wheel for a while. He wanted that too. I finally crossed the Virginia state line at 10 or 11 AM, bearing in mind that the Carolinas and Virginia are lengthy states to drive through. I was so happy when I hit Virginia and had only one more state to go before hitting Maryland. I traveled through Virginia for hours, stopped for gas, ate, and hit rush hour. My legs were killing me, and I had to rest for an hour. Then my menstrual cycle began, but I expected that and was prepared.

At last, I reached Maryland. It took some time to get to Montgomery County, but I made it. I was so happy to arrive! I stopped off at the CVS and then made my way to the house of my "Auntie/Mommy's Sister/Friend." I was very thankful that she opened her home up to us as a rest stop. I felt comfortable there. We talked, and I finally had the time to sit and process everything. Of course, Aunt J and I had a deep talk and agreed that we did not like how my father had handled his illness. I told her that I was very angry with him but understood his "why." I believe that my father did not want to be entangled in a tug of war over where he would spend his final days. Only two years before his passing, he finally decided to marry his third wife legally after thirty years. Although I was very happy about this, I questioned him, asking why he had done it now. Of course, he told me that it was just time to do this, adding that he had a life insurance policy, which he had started less than two years before his passing. He was very different from my mother when it came to finances, probably because no one ever showed him how to manage money—or he hadn't been listening. My grandmothers both had finances and life insurance policies to ensure that things would be done properly when that final day came. My father, likewise, did not want there to be any conflict between his wife and me, as had happened with my mother's third husband. My father absolutely knew that I would have taken in and cared for him, but he made a different choice, which I can truly understand. After spending the night in the Maryland suburbs at Aunt J's house, I finally made it to Beacon, New York. Together, my son and I had made a very long trek, arriving at approximately 4 PM in blistery cold weather that we had not experienced in years. I bundled up, stepped out of the car, and knocked on my father's door. When my father's wife opened it, I grabbed her close to me and hugged and kissed her. I hope that brought her comfort. I knew that I had to be strong for her—it was a must. So I walked in, got myself situated, and immediately said, "What do you need me to do?" The next thing that I knew, we were at the funeral home, where my stepsister was trying to make funeral arrangements.

While I was driving to New York, I'd been asked by phone whether I had enough money for my father's funeral. I said, "Oh my God, no, I do not." If I had, I certainly would have offered. It was a struggle just to get to New York on such short notice. I later learned that it was important to have cash on hand for emergencies. My father's death was a cautionary tale and a lesson that my stepsister and I certainly discussed. We concluded that we did not want this to be "us" on any level. My father's passing was a wake-up call on many levels, and it seemed to take weeks to arrange his funeral. Thankfully, my father was adored by people in his community for all that he gave; that the school district he worked for put out the money for his funeral when they found out, saying that he was too loved to do without closure. Although my father had life insurance, he began his plan too late in the game, so nothing was there financially for us to bury him. I was very upset about this. It took days for the funeral's logistics to be arranged, and I felt restricted to a specific location. Although I was committed to staying with my father's wife at their home, I often went out for a drive to get some air and clear my head. I was on my cycle, tired and out of sorts because of everything that was happening. I wanted to sue someone, but, at the same time, I did not want to challenge anyone because it wasn't the time or place for that. It seemed like forever, but the day of the funeral finally came. The only sibling to show up for my father was his brother, which I found disturbing. However, I did not have the energy to be angry with his siblings. I prayed a lot and simply let things go. I had previously spoken to all of my father's siblings, but one since no one knew where the youngest brother was. Overall, it was a harrowing situation, but I realized that my father had created a family with his wife. The people who loved him most flooded into the funeral home for the service.

Even the mayor of Beacon, New York, Randy Casale, showed up to pay his respects. All of this was mind-blowing for me. I was so proud to see the former students whose lives my father touched during his years of working at the local high school. My father was honored, well-liked, and respected. For many years in the summer, he ran and took on the role of director for a local children's camp, which was sponsored by a church in the community. I knew that his people were present and found myself comforting them.

I spoke at my father's funeral, which was very tough, but I let the world know that he was truly my first teacher, my first playmate, and my first love. I cried, I wept, I held and prayed with people, and I drove my rental car to the train station to pick up my uncle. Afterward, my son, uncle, and I went to the local Panera to eat and talk. I drove my uncle back to the train station and said goodbye to everyone. Then I looked at my father's body one last time and drove back to Maryland to see Aunt J. I was relieved to be in a slightly warmer climate, with more space to be quiet, collect my thoughts, and process my father's passing and funeral. Sadly, my father could not afford to be buried, so they cremated him, which was the complete opposite of what he wanted and believed in doctrinally, coming from a Jehovah's Witness background. Sitting at my kitchen table in 2014, my father had told me that he had argued with my mother about her preference for cremation for many years and vowed that, if she went first, he would not allow it. In the end, my mother opted to be placed in a vault (crypt), and that was indeed her fate. It was like their final wishes for how they were to be laid to rest were swapped and reversed. Sadly, neither parent had wanted me to have any responsibility for their final arrangements. It was clear that I had more say over my father's passing because he wanted it that way. My stepmother and her family were far more respectful and sensitive toward me than my mother's last husband. I am grateful to my father for having those conversations with them because they upheld his desire to treat me as sensitively as possible. It made everything much easier to deal with. As I left Aunt J's house, I thanked her for her hospitality and offered to buy her food, but she would not hear of it and said she was fine. I was very thankful for the large spacious room she gave me. It was very comfortable and provided the quiet peace I needed to grieve and start the healing process, realizing that I had no parents physically on this planet anymore. In a sense, however, my parents' memory became even more real and alive than I could ever imagine. Two very pronounced rays of sun came through the clouds as we were driving home. It was so celestial and divine looking; it almost seemed like something out of a postcard. I felt that the two rays were a symbol of my parents, reunited in heaven and letting us know that everything was going to be alright. God speaks to us through signs, symbols, and His creations. My son and I saw many signs and messages during that road trip, which let us know that all was well. We took comfort in knowing that the Spirit world, the hereafter, and God were all real. As I drove, I looked at my son's face and saw more traces of my father. In fact, looking at my teenage son gave me so much strength because I could see how we live on and continue through our offspring. I just could not believe what I was seeing in my son. In one week of being on the road, I saw a maturity in my son that I had never seen before. He also saw a strength in me that he had never seen before. He kept telling me how remarkably strong that I was, that I was able to cry and still crack a joke through the tears. My son told me that the trip helped him grow spiritually and that he could see the things that I pointed out to him in the Spirit realm to reassure him that God was real. My son's faith in God was deeply enriched and enhanced by the entire journey. Sometimes a spirit of prayer would come over me while I was driving, and I would feel the Holy Spirit overwhelm and comfort me. Sometimes, all I could do was shake my head and grunt because I could not articulate the pain of this loss or how it happened, which seemed so horrible and seemingly unfair to my father. Through it all, however, I trusted God wholeheartedly.

We made a few stops after Maryland, and I was well-rested and able to push through as long as there was daylight. Finally, we made it back to Florida at 11 PM. My leg was killing me, and boy were we glad to be home. Now it was time to start putting the pieces of my life back together and let God create something new in my life. I was two-and-a-half weeks shy of my 40th birthday, with a mysterious lump in my breast and suddenly an orphan. Oh, God, help me! The devil began to attack my mind. I had to fight him while my doctor pleaded with me and sent threatening letters telling me to get a mammogram and a biopsy done because of the lump she had discovered. She thought it was probably a cyst but wanted to be sure. After two months of praying over my breast, turning 40 (a milestone, with neither parent here to see it), and anointing my breast, I was led by the Holy Spirit to start listening to Bishop William Lee Bonner. I believe that I began to see him mentioned in my social-media news feed without realizing why these posts were starting to pop up. I came across a video of Bishop Bonner discussing a testimony about a lump in a woman's breast and how we can take authority over the lump, telling it where to go in Jesus's name. Bonner said that when the doctors are counting you out and have already given you a diagnosis, the ultimate physician, Jesus Christ, has the final say. Although fear can strip you of your faith, we should be bold in faith, knowing that Jesus is a healer. We should speak life and reject illness or a negative prognosis. "Whose report will you believe? We shall believe the report of the Lord."

After listening to him preach, I knew I could take that to the bank and that everything would be just fine. So, I went to have a breast biopsy done. On the day of my biopsy, I wondered where to take myself for my 40th birthday. Twenty years before, my mother had taken me to Las Vegas for my 20th birthday. We probably would have gone back for my 40th birthday if she had been here. As I sat in the office, I saw a home fixer-upper show on the TV; the houses were located in Las Vegas. My spirit was telling me to get ready to go west; this sighting confirmed it immediately. A lady stepped out of the office to call my name. She said, "Lori, my name is Sandy, and I am going to help you get ready for your biopsy today." Well, my mother's name was Saundra, and she hated being called Sandy, but the two names are related. I felt a sort of reassurance from God that I was going to be OK. As any woman who has experienced a biopsy knows, the process is absolutely nerve-racking. I went into the office, Sandy prepared me, and I decided that I would face this and come out of it, alright. After all, I had watched the video of Bishop Bonner saying that all would be well. The technicians and medical professionals seemed pleased after the biopsy needle was inserted into my breast. I could see right away that they were not alarmed or disturbed by what they extracted. Once the procedure was over, they sat me in a room and conversed with me, asking about my weekend plans. They were very upbeat, saying, with a smile, that the doctor will have the results soon. In the meantime, I should enjoy my weekend. Less than two weeks later, the results came in, and because our God is awesome and Bishop Bonner was indeed a true prophet, I was fine. I knew that I could always hang on to the words from Bishop Bonner's mouth; his was a true message that came to pass. Two weeks later, Bishop Bonner passed away on Good Friday, 2015. Less than three months apart, I had lost my natural birth father and my spiritual father. It was just *too* much. Although Bishop Bonner lived 93 wonderful years, did marvelous work, and was certainly not a tragic loss, the timing was all wrong for me. A few weeks earlier, I had learned that the mother of my childhood best friend, Celeste, had also passed away. I spoke to my friend, who had sent lovely flower arrangements for both my parents' funerals, even though she lived in California. I returned the favor by sending flowers and advised her that the Holy Spirit told me to "go west." I had to see her and would come to California, come hell or high water. So, I booked a flight to Las Vegas for my son and me, with a hotel included with the rental car. I was going to celebrate LIFE! God told me to go and get my life, and I also planned to meet and spend time with an online friend I had never met in person. Out of my heart's kindness, I asked my husband whether he wanted to join us on the trip. I had asked this question a week or two later and, of course, by then, the flight we were taking was full. After a few days of deliberation, my husband decided to tag along, so it became a family vacation to look forward to. Although he had to get a different flight, he found one that had roughly the same departure and arrival times. My slanderer/stalker was still watching and tracking me, so I turned my smartphone off for two or three months, feeling as if everything I was trying to do was again being sabotaged. Again, this spirit was looming, and I began to look for a house. I turned forty in February but wanted to have a summer party when we could all get some paid time off, and my son would be home from school.

Scriptural Nugget: Revelation 21:4 NLT

He will wipe every tear from their eyes, and there will be no more death or sorrow or crying or pain. All these things are gone forever."

The Fruits of Our Labor

Before the trip to Vegas, I began to look into buying a new home. I was very frustrated to have reached the age of forty without purchasing my own first home, I was ready, and my credit score was good, so I contacted a wonderful realtor who helped me close the deal on our new home. We were advised that all we needed was to put down 500 dollars for a brand new townhome with stainless steel appliances and granite counters in the kitchen and the bathrooms. It had a spacious lanai, crown molding, three bedrooms, and two-and-a-half bathrooms. I took pictures of my new home in the countryside on Tampa's outskirts and tagged the stalker's friends, showing myself closing the deal in my new kitchen with my realtor. The suspected stalker then posted a picture of a similar-looking "dream kitchen" as something on their wish list. As (Psalm 23:5) says, "You prepare a table before me in the presence of my enemies." Therefore it is so good to hold your peace.

Although I consulted a lawyer, hired a private undercover online investigator, and filed a police report, I did so quietly, never making a big scene publicly on the internet until I was released to make statements by the Holy Ghost. I allowed our "family trip" to Vegas to show God's mighty hand because the suspected stalker had attempted to damage our already damaged marriage. I was not going to let the stalker win. While we were in Vegas, a controversial event took place in the Black Conscious Community with Dr. Umar Johnson, who was exposed for having a relationship with a female stripper. Such behavior seems contradictory in the conscious community where people are supposed to be above exploiting Black women. As soon as the controversy broke, I quickly went online and made a YouTube video out of empathy. Facebook was beginning to turn on Dr. Umar for something that was yet to be established. I knew what it was like for people to turn on you self-righteously without even having the facts. Therefore, I jumped quickly to his defense at the Luxor in Vegas, and my video began to gain massive traction. I started a trend among other more well-known voices in the Conscious Community, who jumped on the bandwagon. Between the video, my new house, and my family vacation, I was BACK after the massive slanderous attack on my character. God got all of the glory because those folks really tried to take me out. The year 2015 started out as a gloomy year but soon began to turn around. The question was, how authentic was this family vacation, which was also a wedding anniversary and celebration of our new home. Was this trip real or simply an effort to "save face" after all the mess? Was I trying to prove that I was indestructible? Yes, I was fuming mad at the devil, and God was blessing me because I stayed quiet. However, mysteriously, two weeks after I returned from my trip, people started giving me funny looks at work, as they had in South Florida. Something was not right. I said to myself, "oh no, not again."

It was the same energy and the same vibe, although I had no concrete proof; a week later, I was let go in a mass layoff of 300 people at various campuses. My boss assured me that I had not done anything wrong, either personally or professionally, and that I was eligible to be re-hired in one year's time. I received severance pay and had to work quickly to find employment by August when I knew my money would run out. My employer knew that we had just purchased a new home, and this was cruel. But I trusted God completely and felt a strange "peace" about this situation, knowing that I would be absolutely fine in the long run. I found a position that I decided to try, even though it was beneath me. I was still thankful for this job and made almost 2,000 dollars in a month's time. It was quick, easy money, which kept us afloat until something better came up. However, I was not happy with the pace or the fact that this job was based on the company's numbers. Although it was fun at first, I began to resent it and knew that it was time for me to make other arrangements. Next, I landed a job that was 54 miles away but more secure. I excelled at this job, which was totally unrelated to education, for four months, and the money helped to sustain me while also providing paid training. It was a lower-level customer-service job, but when you have to pay a new mortgage, you do what needs to be done to ensure that you can keep your house. By the grace of God, we did just that. I went into that role knowing that it was temporary. Given my education and skills, the tide would eventually turn—and it did. While I was there, lower-level co-workers who were jealous of me slashed a tire on my car and broke one of my windows. They did not like me because they thought I was being groomed for promotion, even in the short time I was there. Although I stayed very quiet and minded my own business, most of my colleagues were people who needed either part-time work or a second chance at life. The work was fun, the training was informative, and I later got a job as an advisor, making almost double what I had before, plus overtime. I was back on my feet financially, back in the field of education, and I felt the favor and grace of God in my life again, concerning the provision. God truly sustained us. This transition was a new beginning, which allowed me to gain more experience as a student advisor. The position was not ideal because it involved an intrusive form of advising, which was heavily micromanaged to meet a sales quota, an approach that I strongly disagreed with. Although education is a business, my philosophy prioritizes the industry's human, altruistic side, regarding the business side as the least important aspect.

When students become numbers, the system is compromised. It forces students to go to school or tells advisors that they have to achieve a certain target; if their students do not attend, they will be penalized. It was not true academic advising—it was basically sales and pressurized solicitation. A student could be lying in a hospital bed, and the "advisor" in this institution would make the student log in to an online class, regardless of his or her condition, simply to make the "numbers." I did not go to one of the best schools in the Northeastern region of the United States to force students to attend classes. True Academic Advisors are educators; in a normal college or university setting, the job is quite similar to that of a Guidance Counselor/School Counselor in a P-12 setting. Students come into our office with academic or personal problems that affect them academically, and we provide the knowledge and resources they need to overcome those obstacles. As advisors, we teach students how to navigate the college and inform them of institutional policies and their rights as students. Advisors also integrate academic and career goals to help students discover their life's work. We guide them on the path to success by monitoring their grades, assisting them with academic planning, mapping their progress, and keeping them informed about various tests that they can take to bypass a certain course level or qualify for course credit. We do so much as Academic Advisors. I love this profession because it allows me to be a teacher, counselor, administrator, and so much more to the student population.

At the same time, I finished my doctoral study and encountered a great deal of resistance from my dissertation chair, whom I did not choose. She and I were a total mismatch, even in the field of interest I was pursuing. She was rude to me from the beginning, and it just wasn't working out. The doctoral program offered dissertation workshops but misled students about the process. Students were advised that we would be able to choose the faculty we wanted to work with; this offer never materialized. I was unable to select my dissertation chair even after I successfully passed my comprehensive exam and began a dissertation. Everything in my being was terrified of the process, although I should not have been and did not understand why. Initially, I got a bad vibe from this dissertation chairperson, who was hostile and doubted my ability, straight out of the gate. The situation was very discouraging, indeed. During the very first term of my dissertation work, I wrestled with this problem and struggled immensely. I did not do well because I was confused about the blocks, the timing, and the chairperson's lack of responsiveness to anything that I submitted. On my second try, I had to pay additional money for a retake and realized that I would have to leave my job or find a part-time job that was less stressful and taxing so that I could finish my project. I asked fellow educators and my dissertation mentor (not the chairwoman) about ways to improve my writing, and they agreed that I was now on the right track. I reached out to my dissertation chair and had conferences with her to better understand the process and what she was looking for. I also spent time at dissertation workshops, found an editor, and began to look at the flow of other dissertations. I began to understand the rhythm of a qualitative piece of academic writing, something I came to understand much better as time went on. I attempted to get a work-from-home position that would give me the time to focus on this project, but the money did not add up as promised. Unfortunately, I had to leave that quickly because it put me in a financial bind. Before leaving my job, I had researched this company and found it to be honest. In addition, I had previously applied for a "real" advising job at a local community college in Tampa. It was my second attempt to apply for this position. The floodgates of heaven began to open after a spiritual consecration fast. Many interviews followed, including one at the University of Tampa, which I later turned down because I had finally gotten a position at the community college; I had heard so many wonderful things about it after four months of waiting for a callback. Financially, I was spiraling out of control, which was weird because I'd always been good at managing my money and budgeting. However, when a company says that you will make X amount of money and then delivers less than 1,000 dollars a month, that can be frightening when you are used to making three times that amount or more. So, I took the community college job, which paid less money than what I had earned in many years. I figured, darn it, this is a hell of a lot better than making pennies a day after being promised a livable wage. Although this position was less well paid, I was finally given my own office after six years. I had not had my own office since I was a temporary School Counselor at Brookwood High School in Georgia. Before that, I had not had my own office since my internship at the John Jay College of Criminal Justice in New York. This opportunity also had tremendous benefits, paid time off, paid sick days, paid vacation days, family and medical leave, and tuition reimbursement, as needed. The situation was rather good, and I was thankful to be in this space finally. I prayed many years for this opportunity but did not see the benefits of my graduate training for a long time due to the great recession.

I had begun to file divorce papers in 2014 but had halted that process after my father passed and I was diagnosed with a scary breast lump that turned out to be a benign cyst. Every time I tried to leave my husband, something would frighten me or set me back. Again, the Bible says that God has not given us a spirit of fear but of love, power, and a sound mind, so I am not sure why this pattern seems to occur in my life. However, I feel that it has to do with my mother and how she left her third husband. When my mother finally broke free from him after fourteen years, she was diagnosed with stage-four cancer. I believed subconsciously that something terrible might happen if I took the same step because I always returned to my husband when I was facing loss or felt vulnerable. I am a woman of faith.

    I know that God can do anything because I had seen His miracles and His wondrous works, especially when I stepped out in faith and made radical moves to do what God called me to do. In the end, after buying the house and seeing that my husband did not help me buy new furniture or put any effort or appreciation into creating a home, I realized that nothing would ever make him happy. I wound up spending my own money to furnish "our" new home. I asked for help with the decorating and picture hanging, but we had bare walls for over a year. As a result, I became resentful. The financial abuse continued where I handled most of the expenses, and I no longer felt attracted to my husband. We had had a loveless marriage for the past five years. Sometimes, he tried to penetrate me sexually without my consent while I was asleep. That absolutely enraged me, and I would not let him go any further. I explained that such behavior was considered rape because he was attempting to have sex without the other person's consent. It makes no difference whether I was his wife or not; the sexual act still has to be consensual. We had settled into a long-term pattern of me taking care of most of the household necessities. At the same time, he pocketed his salary and withheld money for food and household furnishings. He always paid his share of the basic household bills, including mortgage/rent, utilities, and other household bills. However, that was not enough. I knew how a male provider is supposed to act; he was not a real provider. My mother allowed a man into our home that did not have a home of his own. This may have impacted my perception of what a provider was supposed to be. I would never have let a man move into my home or any house where I had lived with a previous husband. To me, that seems crazy. Although my mother's third husband was a provider, he took care of her financially, even though she had her own resources. How could I stay in love with someone I didn't respect? With someone who verbally disrespected me; had no empathy; did not want to grow, travel, or expand his mind; and sometimes tried to rough me up physically? I don't believe that God ordained such situations or that we are supposed to endure abuse. Abuse can become a pattern that spills over into every area of our lives. Because this pattern was not dealt with during my childhood years, it followed me through school, where I was bullied; it followed me when I chose controlling and abusive churches or religious organizations. It followed me professionally because the root was still there. Deliverance must occur, and we must place abuse, trauma, the spirit of death, the spirit of sickness, disease, lack, and any other ordeals that plague us at the feet of Jesus. Finally, in 2016, I made my final choice and filed for divorce. This time, I followed through. My finances began to suffer immediately afterward because my husband withdrew his monetary assistance, as he always did when I was not cooperating or seemed to be getting too independent. There was a similar pattern after sexual relations, with his mistreatment of me getting worse after sex. I knew that I did not want to share a marriage bed with him any longer. I felt caught in the same cycle over and over again. It never got any better, and I don't even think he was aware of this pattern, which is weird.

As time progressed, financial challenges arose. At one point, my dissertation seemed to be going well; then, something went terribly wrong. As I grew closer to finishing my dissertation, the chairperson started behaving strangely again. Although I had turned in every required item, she did not respond quickly or explain clearly that this was my final retake. I was under the impression that I had one more opportunity because I had passed the last one. The institution began to drain my resources with totally unnecessary retake classes. My doctoral program partner was going through the same thing, even though we both had GPAs in the 4.0 range. When things suddenly became problematic, I told my friend that something was terribly wrong. I felt that we were being swindled and decided to drop out before things got crazy or my pockets were completely empty. My friend held on, and I returned, only to persevere, seemingly do well, and then get dropped. I often wonder if that was a political backlash because I was a former employee. Later, I realized that the school was having financial trouble. They began to do all kinds of crazy financial things to students around that time to get more money out of us and keep the school afloat. Sure enough, the school closed less than a year after I discontinued the dissertation program. I could have reapplied and returned to finish, but I opted not to, and I am so glad that I didn't. The most painful aspect of this experience was the amount of debt that I accrued in a predatory program that gave me nothing apart from experience. I experienced sorrow for about sixteen hours, but twenty-four hours later, I was filled with optimism and started to feel better. I knew and still know that I will come out of this and that my student loan will disappear or be eliminated in Jesus's name. I applied for the public-service loan forgiveness program for educators and government workers and the income-based repayment plan, which allows students to certify with their employers every couple of months. After ten years of service, the lender will calculate all of your 120 payments and forgive the remainder of your loan. The longer I live, the more I realize how quickly ten years can pass. I have also applied for borrower defense relief. It can take up to two years to get a decision, but if you can prove that your school deceived you, they will forgive your loan. We do not have to remain trapped in a never-ending cycle of debt. I did not grow up in a household with a "broke" mindset. As a child, I never heard anyone declare, "I'm broke." I do not come from a place of generational poverty on my mother's side. I never had a "that's just the way it is" mentality. Instead, I saw great prosperity and good financial management in my childhood. Even when we get into a rut, we must know that the situation is temporary. As long as we have life, health, strength, cognition, and the power of God, we can get out of any bad situation in Jesus's name. For the Word of the Lord in (1 Corinthians 10:13) says, "he will show you a way out so that you can endure." I don't claim to be stuck; I do not claim obstacles; I don't claim that I can't; I do not profess to lack anything. Instead, I claim abundance and believe Psalm 84:11 (AMP), which says, "For the Lord God is a sun and shield; The Lord bestows grace and favor *and* honor; No good thing will He withhold from those who walk uprightly."

Scriptural Nugget: Proverbs 22:24-25 NLT

"Don't befriend angry people or associate with hot-tempered people, or you will learn to be like them and endanger your soul."

The Rededication

During 2014, I began to sincerely rededicate myself to Christ, having grown slack since 2011. I'm not sure whether the scandal at New Birth weakened my resolve. I didn't think so at the time, but perhaps it did a little, and I just wasn't aware of it. I was mature enough to handle that crisis and did not run away when it happened. Instead, I was heartbroken for my Bishop and deeply hurt. When the slander and confusion occurred online, it sent me right back into prayer. The doors began to open, and my prayer life re-ignited. I think God used that whole ordeal and attack to reel me back into the place He desired me to be because I was straddling philosophies and inserting rationalism into my Christian philosophy. Most people don't realize that I never served "other Gods;" I simply chose to see the Creator through a "cultural lens," as opposed to a traditional perspective. After everything I had been through in recent years, I decided to rededicate myself fully to pursuing the presence of The Lord Jesus Christ, something I had honestly never stopped doing. I never stopped listening to Christian sermons or praying.

To say that I stopped praying in English or tongues would be ludicrous. I never ever stopped communicating with God, Almighty. After I had been in Florida for years, searching for a church, the Spirit of the Lord directed me toward a church in Orlando. I finally went on a Saturday night, and the rest is history. I knew as soon as I walked into that church that I was truly home. The message preached that night was timely. It was a week before the Christmas season, and I was determined to return to "my new church," which I did one week later. From that point on, I never stopped. In March 2017, I officially joined by taking the new-members class. Fast forward to the end of March 2018, after making the decision to not return to the previous doctoral program. I prayed, researched, and began to take steps to ensure that this academic setback did not take me into the depths of sorrow. My prayers were successful, and it did not. I found a Doctor of Education (Ed.D; not pastoral) program at a college I had never even heard of, which had an accelerated program track. Students could earn an Ed.D degree in a hybrid format: half online and half in person. I said to the Lord God: "I need a program where I can be seen and known by my professors so that this never happens again. I am not just another number." I said, "Lord, I need something affordable." I did not know how much money I had left. Someone advised me that I had maxed out of Financial Aid. I completed the application process for this beautiful and highly respected institution, was invited for an interview, and, thirty days after leaving my last school, was accepted into a new doctoral program at a reputable institution, with fantastic rankings in *U.S. News and the Princeton Review*! God works amazingly fast! I was afraid that no funding would be available, although the Financial Aid and Admissions representatives had both pushed me to register. I told them that I needed to know what money was available because I did not want a bill. Once you have been scammed, you don't trust many people or organizations because you have been burned and betrayed.

Being indecisive, I let this idea go for a year and assumed that I was finished, following a review of my student financial record. I prayed and said, "Lord, here is what I will do. I will surrender my dream of completing my doctorate and do what you want me to do." I still have not made a decision concerning my continuation of doctoral studies, but at least I have more options. At the church that I had joined, I completed a foundations class that would give me access to all church ministries. I told God, "I will do this by committing to fifteen weeks and then serve you faithfully in the church and forget about my dream. At this point, I was still making 12,000 dollars less per year than I used to make. When I surrendered, my job increased my salary by 12,000 dollars, paid retroactively. This return was truly a miracle. I said to God, "That's why you told me not to move from this position because you had this in store for me." Finally, I was able to pay some bills. I had canceled a trip to Ethiopia because I couldn't save enough money in time. The Holy Spirit told me to cancel it, and, about five months later, the same Ethiopian airline experienced a fatal crash. I was refunded most of the money I'd spent, and when I received it, Holy Spirit said: "You obeyed, and now you are going to book two trips, one to Ghana, West Africa and a cruise to Mexico with your son to see the Mayan temples in Chichen Itza." So, I finally went to West Africa to see the home of my ancestors. For me, this was a dream come true.

Scriptural Nugget: Romans 8:38-39 NLT

"And I am convinced that nothing can ever separate us from God's love. Neither death nor life, neither angels nor demons, neither our fears for today nor our worries about tomorrow—not even the powers of hell can separate us from God's love. No power in the sky above or in the earth below—indeed, nothing in all creation will ever be able to separate us from the love of God that is revealed in Christ Jesus our Lord."

Those Deep, Dark Family Secrets

The amazing trip to Ghana occurred a few months after my father's half-sister asked if I wanted to take a DNA test for family tracing and personal connectivity purposes. I said, "sure." For years, I had wanted to do this with my mother and father before they passed, but the kits were very expensive. My father always said he was willing to do this, and now his sister was asking me to take one, even though we had never discussed it. My aunt bought kits for both of us, and we took the DNA tests. She received her results a few days before I did. I discovered, from the original results, that I was 26% Ghanaian. I knew that I was about 20% Caucasian since one of my great-great-great-grandparents was known to be White (my maternal great-great-great-grandfather), and I probably had a White ancestor on my West Indian side. I also found an indigenous piece indicating Native American genes; that did not surprise me either. However, the huge surprise was noticeable but confusing. I shared over 600 centimorgans of DNA with my father's half-sister, but a whopping 1,171 centimorgans with a total stranger who was unrelated to my father's sister. Centimorgans measure the amount of DNA you share with another person. Who could this mystery person be?

I reached out and emailed her. We began to talk, and yes, she was from New York and part of the same generation as my mother, just six years younger. My father's sister, who had purchased the kit, said that she shared no DNA with the person I described, suggesting a connection on my mother's side of the family. I turned this over every which way in my head, wondering who this person could be related to. I kept coming up with uncertainties because my mother specifically asked her father before he passed away, "Daddy, are you sure that there is nobody else out there, other than me, as your child?" He replied, "not that I know of." For some reason, my mother told me this story several times. I remembered it because my grandfather was a notorious womanizer. My grandmother had publicly accused my grandfather in the *Amsterdam News* in 1947 for philandering with his client, the legendary Jazz singer Maxine Sullivan. It was a whole big mess and an "Uproar in Harlem." My grandmother sued my grandfather and Maxine Sullivan and in 1950, the mystery lady with the DNA sample was born. It just so happens that this dear, sweet lady was not just a born-again believer (born in Queens, New York, which made me consider the Smiths and Terrys on my mother's side), but now lived in Florida, just like me! When she emailed me and told me where she lived, I almost threw my computer across the room. I continued to research possible connections; she was quiet for a time, and I did not hear from her. Finally, I found a centimorgans chart online that broke down percentages and the various relationships one could have with a person with her shared DNA . Finally, I said to myself: "Oh my goodness! I think I've got it." I asked her to send another picture of herself so that I could look at her again from another angle. She obliged, and some bells went off for me because she resembled my mother's first cousins on her father's side, according to my recollections (I had not seen them since childhood). I said to her, "I think I am your niece." I then emailed her a picture of my grandparents looking stunning and said, "This is my grandfather, Elbert J. Terry." She asked me, "was he just known as Terry?" I said he was. She said, "I was always told that he was my father." Boom!! I said, "Let's talk,"; so we did and had a great conversation.

We had to catch up on 44 years of my life that we missed sharing because of a pregnancy that my grandfather kept concealed when he was separated from my grandmother. Now, my mother's stories all made sense. My mother said she could never understand why; whenever her father called the house when she was growing up, her mother started raging and screaming, "I hate him!" in the background when he asked to speak to my mother. Maxine Sullivan bought my mother a dress as a peace offering, but my grandmother refused to accept it. Her disdain for everything "Terry" continued. Although my grandmother calmed down when she remarried, her feelings toward my grandfather never changed. My mother did not understand that deep-seated hatred, but I believe that she knew that something was seriously wrong because my grandmother became irrational at the mention of his name. At that point, the relationship between my grandmother and grandfather had been severed for a long time. My mother did not understand why they were still arguing for so many years after the fact. Fast forward to 2018, and my newfound aunt and I began to talk every day. She became an avid family-history researcher, using all of the online databases on the ancestry website to go back in time and collect information. She was very accurate in her findings, staying up until the wee hours of the morning deep in the rabbit hole of research. My aunt was able to make some wonderful, accurate connections. For example, following my suggestion, she finally managed to obtain a copy of her birth certificate. I had told her that it would probably include some important information, such as an address, which could tell her who her biological parents were. Her birth certificate indicated an address in Queens, New York, the borough that my grandfather lived in before he passed away. My aunt plugged this address into the Internet and discovered the owner of that house: my grandfather's first cousin, Wesley Terry. My grandfather must have used this address because he was staying there—or perhaps he wanted to leave a clue for his child. My only question (and my Aunt's present dilemma) is who her birth mother is or was. For some odd reason, I feel that the answer is right under our noses.

My aunt seems to think her mother may have been Maxine Sullivan. My aunt Angela has reached out to Maxine's offspring, who replied that she did not think this was true and, if it were, it would've been an uncomfortable situation. I told my aunt that Maxine's daughter might assume she was trying to get something from the family. I knew this wasn't my aunt's intention, but people tend to think that way. Maxine Sullivan passed away from a seizure in 1987, the year my grandmother's first brain tumor was discovered and surgically removed. I can recall my mother saying to me: "Damn it, Lori, I had questions for Maxine! I wanted to sit down and talk to her about some things." I was twelve-and-a-half years old and did not have the insight to push my mother into further dialogue, even though I felt she wanted to talk to me in-depth. She had no known siblings, and I, too, was an only child. I imagine that she had no one else to talk to about the family apart from her cousin Larry, who was not a stable person or someone she could talk to regularly. I truly believe that my mother knew (or had heard) something during her childhood, perhaps involving the existence of a sister. I know that during two critical times in her life, her mother's passing and her own battle with cancer, she said, "Lori, I wish I had a sister to help me through this." My mother did not say that she wanted a sibling; she specified "sister." I said, "Mommy, you have me. Aren't I enough support?" She said, "Yeah, but it would be different." I guess she also meant someone to look out for her child if she wasn't there. My mother used to love the movie *"The Body Guard,"* starring Whitney Houston and Kevin Costner. Her favorite line from the movie was when Kevin Costner's character, Frank, was asked, "What are you afraid of the most?" Frank replies, "not being there." My mother shared that story to let me know that the most painful part of her battle with the disease was the fear of "not being there" for the people she loved, who needed her.

Even though my mother's physical connection is gone, I can honestly say that modern science has enabled me to hold on to my loved ones and discover new ways of reconnecting to parts unknown. To solidify the DNA connection I shared with my mother's half-sister, I searched for my mother's two first cousins, Lelar and Joan, who are sisters. I prayed that they were still alive and able-bodied. I went through the white pages online and found Joan still living in New York. I had not seen my elder cousins since I was twelve years old, and I felt terrible that they were so disconnected from my mother. In fact, no one had told them that my mother was gone nine years after her passing. They were left out because I was barred from making arrangements at my mother's funeral. If her husband had not totally disrespected me, the right people would have been notified. I had to catch Joan upon my life, and she had to catch me up on hers. Long story short, I told her that I had discovered a long-lost relative who had been adopted by some friends of my grandfather in Long Island. Joan said to me, "Lori, I have a DNA kit sitting right here that I have not used." I said, "You have got to be kidding!" She said, "no," and I said, "let's make sure you have the right DNA kit—is it ancestry. com for sure?" She said, "Yes," and I thought this is unbelievable! I had to push and prod her for a few weeks, but finally, she submitted the test, and yes, she and my aunt Angela were classified as first cousins when the results came in; Joan is also my mother's first cousin as well, confirming that my aunt was really my aunt and indeed my mother's half-sister.

RAISING ME: A STORY OF GOD'S REDEMPTIVE GRACE AND POWER

Sadly, my mother never had a chance to meet her sister, although there is a part of me that truly believes that both of my parents got in God's ear since I know that their greatest fear was leaving their only baby girl alone on this planet. Why did my father's half-sister call me with such urgency to take this test? She did not know that my father and I had planned to do it together before he passed and missed the chance to do so. My father's half-sister directed me to my mother's half-sister through DNA ; to intensify the scenario, cousin Joan's sister lives forty minutes from Aunt Angela here in Florida! Only God could arrange this, with my two parental angels making requests. I thought I had no biological family in Florida, but I have two wonderful women I was able to bring together. Aunt Angela never realized that her blood first cousin lived forty minutes south of her, while her niece was two hours north—all on the same Florida coast. It's a fantastic story and a real-life miracle.

I planned my trip to Ghana and researched the country extensively, discovering places where I wanted to go and stay at for less than 1,500 dollars. For this journey to Ghana, I had to get the yellow fever vaccination. After calling all around Florida to find the lowest price, I found the shot for 150 dollars, far less than the standard price of 300 dollars, in the town where my Aunt Angela lived. As my aunt and I had never met, I figured that this was an opportunity to meet her while I was in the region finally. We planned our meeting, and she cooked a nice meal, and I was ready! When I pulled up at her house and knocked on her door, I said a prayer. She opened the door, and I said, "awwww." I really felt my mother's spirit with us. I hugged and kissed her in the same manner that my mother would have done. The most painful part about this new connection was that my mother could not join the reunion. However, I feel that she is a part of things, just not in the physical sense of enjoying her nieces and nephews. I now understand why I pleaded with her for so many years to end certain things in her life and fully accept Christ as Lord. I saw her fate as a child in a dream, and I thank God for the warnings, chastisement, and correction by way of the Word of God (Hebrews 12:6).

Before leaving the country for Ghana, I went to see my Aunt Angela and spent the night with her. I told her that I would not dare leave the country without saying goodbye. We hung out, talked, and went to breakfast, where Uncle Rob, her husband, joined us. They prayed over me, and I went home. A day later, I was on my way to the Motherland, Ghana. I went to the airport with my son, who dropped me off and waited with me until it was time to board the flight. I thought about and discussed the steps I had taken to make this trip happen at the airport. I remembered how God truly made it happen financially, as I had just filed for bankruptcy due to years of financial abuse and the withholding of funds on the part of my ex-husband. Still, I was able to plan, research, and stay at a beautiful, large Airbnb house off the coast of Ningo Prampram in Ghana, known as Coconut Pointe. All by myself, I researched where to go and what to see within a reasonable budget. On my first day in Africa, I became very depressed and wanted to go home. My menstrual cycle was coming, but it was more than that—I also realized that I was having a spiritual response to the region and the territory. Sometimes, we can feel poverty and sorrow in places that we have never seen or experienced. Those of us who can sense it must pray if we are receptive to the Holy Spirit. I prayed heavily in Africa and spent the last two days of my vacation locked in my room in prayer, as God had instructed me to do.

This vacation was supposed to celebrate my graduation from the school that eventually closed down and shut me out when I ran out of funds. While I waited, I went to work in the church. The favor of God was on me significantly as I sat in my Foundations classes, preparing to serve in ministry at my church. One of the instructors moved me forward into teaching because of the gift the Holy Spirit had given me. I was delighted and humbled by this promotion. I asked God to guide me and told Him that I would serve Him and do His will if the school was a no-go. I set out along this path.

Meanwhile, I was still receiving text messages and emails from the University, asking me if I still wanted to attend, almost a year after my application. So I stretched out on faith and registered for the class, and praise God, the money was there! Then I went back to waiting. God said, not yet.

After all of the adversity I experienced earlier in the year, I found my awesome aunt and suddenly began to develop new-found strength, knowing that I had family in the state of Florida. I spent my first Thanksgiving with my mother's sister, and it was great. For starters, she served shrimp with cocktail sauce, a dish that my mother also loved. My son was very touched by his first visit to his great aunt. Through her, he also gained a pleasant memory of his grandmother. The first time I visited her, she made quiche and a salad, as my mom used to do back in the 1980s. Many little details showed me that this lady was very similar to my mother. There are some likes, dislikes, and behaviors that you just can't fabricate; some things are genetic. When I began talking with Joan and Lelar, my mother's two first cousins, I noticed that Angela, Lelar, and Joan had similar vocal intonations as family members often do. The fact that they were not raised together but still had such similar voices was amazing. In fact, we ALL have a similar vocal intonation. We made a plan to get together for Christmas 2018, but tragedy struck. My cousin (my aunt's son) was tragically killed in a motorcycle accident. His untimely loss put a damper on our reunion. During this time of shock and grief for my aunt and her family, I did my best to offer as much financial support and emotional support as I could. A mother never recovers from the loss of her child; that goes against the natural order of things. I gave my aunt space and time she needed to grieve, tie up loose ends, and hold a funeral service out of state back in New York. So, I wound up spending my first Christmas with my mother's two first cousins, Lelar and Joan, in Naples, Florida. Joan came down from New York to be with her sister in Naples, and I loved my time there. It was a truly life-changing experience. Their stories inspired me as they are extremely accomplished women whose professional lives have been noted in the New York Times. Another powerful coincidence was that Lelar and Aunt Angela both worked at the same social-services agency without knowing that the other existed. God is just absolutely amazing, and when He does something, He does it well. As this story began to unfold, I was in shock every step of the way because there were just too many parallels, despite time, space, and separation. DNA is really powerful.

Later that year, I had taken my son on a cruise to the Mayan ruins in Chichen Itza, Cozumel, Mexico, for his birthday. We had a blast, and I was so happy that I could share those moments with him during a field trip that was both educational and adventurous. I almost felt like *Indiana Jones in the*

Temple of Doom. It was good to spend quality time with my son. The New Year was fast approaching, and I was able to spend Christmas Eve with Joan, Lelar, her husband Henry, daughter Dana, granddaughter Jada, and her mother-in-law. I felt like I was home and had a truly glorious time, even though it was my first Christmas with blood relatives, with whom I had never spent a single Christmas with in my life. I was very happy to be welcomed and embraced in that lovely environment. Despite everything I had lost, God had restored me beyond my wildest imagination. After I lost my mom, dad, and marriage, God gave me an aunt; I did not know I had and reunited me with family.

I am forever thankful that I could help my aunt connect with her biological father's family. Now, if I could only help her discover her birth mother, that would be awesome. I trust that everything will manifest itself in due time. We concluded that people went to severe extremes to conceal my aunt's birth, probably for a good reason. In the 1950s, a child born out of wedlock was tainted with the stigma of illegitimacy. When my aunt was born, her father was separated from his wife but still legally married. As my mother always said, "she waited for him," when describing her parents' separation, which lasted for six years until my mother was nine. In 1953, my grandparents' divorce was finalized, and they were legally divorced, according to my mother. At the end of her life, my mother told me that her mom stopped hugging her after the divorce. I could not believe it, and I was hurt and devastated for my mother. Her story proved that my suspicions were correct: she really had been emotionally and psychologically abused by her mother. If families don't identify these damaging behavioral patterns, become aware of them, and lay them at the feet of our Lord and Savior, they are doomed to repeat them generationally. By January 2019, my bankruptcy was discharged, and my previous debts (apart from the student loans) were dismissed in court. The loans were astronomical, but they did not frighten me because God has a method and a plan in all things. We must trust that He would not lead us to experiences without providing a means of escape, even if I lacked the knowledge to plan differently. When our intentions are good and pure, God does not let His children suffer unfairly or unjustly. It is simply not his way or His will. During this time, I had to promptly pay the court clerk, at the rate of 2000 dollars, because she said I had too much in assets; even after the discharge, I still owed money. When it seems as if your finances are being tampered with, given that you are pretty responsible about bills and budgeting, the reality of financial abuse becomes very realistic and can no longer be denied. I decided that I would never stand for or tolerate neglect, abuse, disrespect, or dishonor ever again. More than a year had passed since my second divorce from the same man was finalized, and I knew that the marriage was indeed over this time. I was never going back to my ex-husband as a wife. The cursing, profanity, insults, and name-calling in front of our son showed me that he was neither psychologically intact nor had the conscientiousness to make sure that his behavior did not negatively impact his son.

I have had to talk with my son about healthy relationship dynamics and what relationships should be like so that he does not repeat his father's behavior. I do not want any young woman to endure what I went through, especially at my son's hands. As his mother, I would be horrified if that ever occurred. My son is currently in counseling, and we are working to break these cycles and patterns in our family so that we can have happy, healthy relationships in the future. Dysfunctionality does not have to define our descendants; this toxic behavior will be eliminated and purged from us, never to return, by the blood of Jesus Christ. Thankfully, my son has a best friend whose parents have acted as a template, modeling healthy African-American family dynamics with a man who provides for his wife and respects her. My son is aware of the contrast between their relationship and that of his own parents, and we have discussed that in-depth.

After two years, I still found myself struggling to leave my marriage physically. For more than two years, my ex-husband and I continued to live under the same roof, in different spaces, and with little conversation. We only discussed our son and bills that needed to be paid. Leaving is the hardest part. It was difficult to sell a house that I considered to be "my house," "my idea," and "my blessing"—not his. However, I got to a place where I had to start over. Living together would continue to send the message that his treatment of me was OK. It would justify his flawed belief that I wasn't able to make it without him. I knew that God could and would provide. However, studies have shown that it sometimes takes up to seven attempts for women who have been in long-term abusive relationships to leave physically. I had to get to a place where I no longer believed the lies of the enemy of my soul and had unshakeable faith, trusting God for all of my life's breakthroughs. I eventually decided that leaving was the right thing to do, and God miraculously removed him from the household. I decided that I would not spend the rest of my life being miserable, in a loveless marriage or relationship with someone I could not even have a conversation with—someone I had nothing in common with, who was not even my friend. I could not remain with someone who was disconnected from reality when it came to our relationship dynamic. I had cried for too many years over something that was never going to change. I put entirely too much effort into cohabiting and merely existing together. Every time we had a joint bill that was heading toward collections, he would leave it to me and try to ruin my credit rating. Everything he did was spiteful. In return, I began to leave everything he created as a mess in the house for him to clean up instead of being obsessive about neatness, as my mother and grandmother were. I refused to clean up after him on any level. He was on his own during the last few years of our marriage and afterward when we were divorced but cohabiting. We did not have any sexual relations during our post-divorce cohabitation period, as I was no longer attracted to my ex-husband. My attraction for him physically had disappeared many years ago. He simply did not realize or make the connection that the root cause was his treatment of me—some women are being abused or mistreated sleep with their partners. I don't know how they do it. Perhaps they are so fearful of being physically hurt that they are willing to continue having sexual relations. I'm just not able to do that, and my body would not respond.

For many years, going back to my late twenties, I had suffered from symptomatic fibroids. It was first noted that I had this condition when I was twenty-seven, and I was diagnosed at thirty. For years, I went to many gynecologists who had told me that I was not a lost cause and that my uterus could be saved. Only one or two doctors believed that my uterus could not be preserved, but I waited for fourteen years before attempting a myomectomy.

I thank God I did this because technology changed during those years, and myomectomies are now far less invasive. The surgery can be performed as a same-day procedure, with patients going home a couple of hours after. The large fibroid that was most concerning was removable, along with five other fibroids. I returned to work three weeks later because I finally had job security and a good family and medical leave plan. I knew that I would not be replaced if I took time off of work to recuperate. Amazingly, my ex-husband wanted to work as usual during my procedure, although I had asked him to be there for his son in the waiting room because this was a serious procedure. Thankfully, he stayed and tried to help during the recovery process, but my son was very much in charge. He was my biggest helper during this time. The time off allowed me to spend more time in prayer; it built up my inner man with strength and a renewed faith. I cried, prayed, slept, and ate. People called and checked in on me. I was well-rested, feeling more youthful and rejuvenated than I had in years. Two weeks later, I purchased a new car because my engine gave out in the old one.

Strangely, during my time off, I had hardly driven my car. Instead, my son had driven the car to and from work. However, everything operates in divine time, and God wanted to show Himself mightily because I had just had the bankruptcy discharged. I was able to get a brand-new 2019 vehicle with absolutely no money down! As Lamentations (3:23) says, "Great is his faithfulness; his mercies begin each morning, afresh." God proved Himself faithful in the midst of illness, financial depletion, and life's changes. I give Him the praise and all of the glory. At this point, I was feeling strong enough to make other moves and began a series of "can do" moments when things you thought you "could not do" begin to happen.

Oddly, I had another diagnosis this year: that I needed a parathyroidectomy. I had no idea what my parathyroid was. I knew about my thyroid, but this was something different. No one knows what causes hyperparathyroidism. Researchers speculate, but there is nothing concrete. The parathyroid consists of four glands, each the size of a tiny grain of rice. They sit behind the thyroid and can become enlarged. If one gland becomes enlarged, it can throw off the entire body by triggering it to over-produce calcium, which can gradually make you very ill. I did not understand why I still had fatigue, forgetfulness, and physical pain after my surgery—this was why. If left untreated, hyperparathyroidism disease can wreak havoc on the body over time.

I was health-conscious for nearly two decades, and I have cared for my body to the best of my ability. I did not understand how all of this could happen to me. I realized that much of it was spiritual and a manifestation of everything I'd been through over the past fifteen years. On average, doctors discover hyperparathyroidism years after developing in the body, which is a scary thought. I also believe that the more I pursue God and His plan by serving and searching with a vengeance for his presence and purpose in my life, the less the devil is pleased. The surgery for hyperparathyroidism takes no more than twenty minutes, and you can go home an hour or two after your surgery. My son brought me to the hospital, waited with me, and drove me home again. The pain was minimal, and a day later, I finished decorating my home with holiday lights. God is faithful and just; He is a healer, restorer, and provider of good things to those who love Him. I had a fantastic holiday season with a powerful New Year's Eve spent in prayer and powerful praise. The Spirit of the Lord fell, and chains were broken and yokes destroyed.

Here I stand, at a crossroads in my life, not knowing what is next. I trust God to provide a strategy for my next steps, and I am not just floating into the next phase of my life. When there is a critical need, crisis, or emergency, we should never be ashamed to ask for help and seek it. Counseling and psychotherapy are useful coping tools. I am fighting for the rest of my life, which is the time to make critical decisions about how I plan to spend it. Drama-free, with peace and contentment—that is my goal. If that means having less for some time, then so be it. We must know when to shift, when to transition, when to move, and when to yield; we must obey the Holy Spirit and discern the difference between God's voice and man's. This is a time for prayer, fasting, and listening because time spent communing with God is the most valuable time we can spend on earth. Having the clarity and directional focus that only comes from God almighty is what matters most. Jesus said, "my sheep know my voice and a stranger they will not follow" (John 10:5).

We have to be willing to follow Jesus, trusting Him even when we can't trace Him, knowing that He leads and guides us every step of the way in His direction. We must understand that God knows exactly what is best for us, and He has the best plan for our lives. My ex-husband eventually moved out, has started life over in another region, and I kept the house.

Scriptural Nugget: Luke 8:17 NLT

"For all that is secret will eventually be brought into the open, and everything that is concealed will be brought to light and made known to all."

What Is Love?

There are times where we are inspired by love and driven by God's love. When you love someone who loves you back, it becomes genuinely motivational. The love we seek is often found within; someone once said that the love you feel when you are falling in love is nothing but the love already inside you. The spark of love that seems to be triggered by an outside source is the spark that already exists within us. It just needs to be reignited. The Bible gives us four types of love: "The Hebrew word *yada* and the Greek word *eros* are the words used to indicate sexual love. In Genesis 38, Judah makes love with a woman he assumes is a prostitute. In the original Hebrew of Verse 26, the word is *yada*, meaning 'to know and in this context, 'to know carnally' or 'to have sexual intercourse with.' In the New Testament, the Greek word *eros* is not found because there is no context in which it might be used" (Bible Gateway, Source). The second type of love is the brotherly love that exists between close friends, regardless of gender. Here, there is no sexual connotation; it is the love for and by a friend. The Hebrew word is *ahabah*, which is used to describe David and Jonathan's love in I Samuel 20:17. The Greek word for brotherly love or affection is *phileo*, used to refer to friendship in John 15:19, Romans 12:10, and Hebrews 13:1.

The Hebrew word used to denote family or tribal love is once again *ahabah*, indicating a deep affection; the greek word is *storge*. We find *ahabah* throughout the Old Testament because of its broad range of meanings. still, the Greek word *storge* is only found in the new Testament as a part of a compound word (e.g., it's combined with *phileo* in 2 Timothy 3:3 (Bible Gateway, Source). Finally, the Hebrew word is chesed, and the Greek word agape, which is used to express the kind of love that God demonstrates toward His elect. *Chesed* is translated as "steadfast love" or "loving-kindness."

An excellent example of *chesed* is found in Numbers 14:18, "The Lord is slow to anger and abounding in steadfast love, forgiving iniquity and transgression" (Numbers 14:18, ESV). "God's *chesed* love is why He never gives up on those He has adopted as His children. Throughout the Old Testament, God's people repeatedly fell into idolatry and sin, yet He always preserves a remnant; He never gives up on His people. The reason is His *chesed* love."

A similar idea can be found in the New Testament with the Greek word *agape*. *Agape* love is the goodwill and benevolence of God shown in self-sacrifice and an unconditional commitment to a loved one. *Agape* is similar to *chesed* in that it is steadfast, regardless of circumstances. *Agape* love is the kind of love we must have for God in fulfillment of the greatest commandment (Matthew 22:37). Jesus wants to instill *agape* in His followers, as we serve others through the power of the Holy Spirit (Matthew 22:39; John 13:34)." Source: (Gotquestions.org, 2019). The ideal love that we in the Body of Christ strive to have is altruistic and more along the lines of *agape* love, which is unconditional, and *phileo* love, which is brotherly love and often displayed in the Body of Christ among believers. Ultimately, the love that we have for one another is how the world defines us as Christians (John 13:35).

The relationships that we display with each other sometimes spill over into the relationships that we have with those in the world around us. We have the power to shine the light of Christ in the face of a dark and dying world, where the love of many is waxing cold because we are in the last and evil days. This simply means the end of an *age, epoch,* or *eon,* as the word, age is translated from the Greek, as found in Matthew (28:20). However, there will be a new heaven and a new earth, where all things will be made new, as Revelation (24:4–5) states: "He will wipe away every tear from their eyes, and there will be no more death or mourning or crying or pain, for the former things have passed away." "And the One seated on the throne said, Behold, I make all things new." Love makes all things new. When we think of love in modern society, we often think about eros love, described above as romantic love. We need this and initial attraction when we are considering marriage.

However, it is *storge* love that keeps a marriage together because *storge* love is more familial in nature, designed to hold a union together. I used to have very deep discussions with my mother about why marriages fail and why the divorce rate is so high, and why her own marriages failed. I said, "Ma, so many people marry for lust and confuse it with love." People don't marry just to create a family; they marry because they want a "lover for life" and don't think about the other components that make a marriage.

Partnership, friendship, and companionship are all wonderful, but our motives for getting married in modern society are skewed because we do not focus on family. We do not marry for "family" or to be a family; people get married to be lovers. When the passion wears off, we think we are no longer in love because we perceive eros love as the only form of love that we are supposed to feel in a union. I went into both of my marriages with the forethought of family, which I think is why, despite differences, our unequal yoking and incompatibility at every level (spiked with verbal and emotional abuse, remarriage, and codependency), we were able to stay married for so long.

The quality that attracted me to my ex-husband was the family cohesion that he publicly displayed. It turned out not to be real—all that glitters is not gold. I have learned that I am a woman who loves too much, gives too much, and over-extends herself too quickly. Observing my mother's relationship dynamic with her last husband, I have learned to give too much to the point of depletion. I believed that I had conquered this through three years of therapy and time spent fighting for my deliverance, and yes, I did well overall. I exceeded my own parents' expectations and quite a few of my own. God has been good to me because I aim to love the Lord as He commanded in Deuteronomy (6:5), "And you must love the LORD your God with all your heart, all your soul, and all your strength." When we love God, feast on His word and what it says about us, we tune out other voices that tell us otherwise. We allow ourselves to be shaped by who God says we are. What demonstrates how important we are to the Lord and how much God loves us is the moment when He says, "we are the apple of His eye." (Psalm 17:8; Proverbs 7:2; Zechariah 2:8). "We are fearfully and wonderfully made."

(Psalm 139:14), and "the very hairs on our head are numbered by our God" (Luke 12:7). Who wouldn't want a God like that who carefully crafted us in His image and redeemed us unto Himself because He loved us so much that He could not live without us? That's an amazing love that goes beyond anything we can comprehend.

The greatest sacrifice is that "God so loved the world that He gave His only begotten son, that whosoever believes in Him should not perish but have everlasting life" (John 3:16). Knowing how much God loves us ignites something within us, causing us to not only love Him but also to "love others, but we also love ourselves." As Mark (12:31) says, "Love your neighbor as yourself." The key is to love ourselves. If we do this, we will love others from a God-centered place that is pure and without ulterior motives. Agape love will result in healthy, long-lasting relationships, viewed from a God perspective. This love extends mercy and grace; it provides healthy self-sacrificial behavior and encourages us to prefer another over ourselves (Philippians 2:3). "Do nothing from selfishness or empty conceit but with humility of mind regard one another as more important than yourselves." It is so easy to become engulfed in this modern age of selfish love, consumed with the self and narcissistic in nature. We seem to think that this is normal. Today's society has a perverted and distorted view of the truth of God's love and what it looks like. Temporary emotions are proof that love is not a feeling or a fleeting emotion but an action word. We know that a person loves us by what they do and how they demonstrate that they love us. By staying so long in an abusive relationship that wasn't always bad, did I lack self-love? Did I have self-esteem issues that were rooted in the verbal, psychological, and emotional abuse that I received as a child? I thought I had worked this out, but sometimes we overestimate where we are in Christ and our development.

Given all the prayer, time, therapy, and deliverance I put in, perhaps this cycle or piece of my saga should never have happened. However, I don't think I should be so hard on myself or undermine the Holy Spirit's work in my life. Considering all that I endured, my life could have turned out a whole lot worse. I could have stayed with the wrong crowd, never gone beyond the GED, or remained in the Bronx. Although I did not live in a bad part of the Bronx, the neighborhood was changing, and I knew that my current mindset was no longer compatible with my former interests. I have genuinely forgiven my mother's ex-husband and moved on. I have taken the advice that my father gave me during the last few months of his life about how to deal with what remained of my own life. I trusted my dad's advice because I knew there were no ulterior motives or manipulative underpinnings in his willingness to give counsel.

For this reason, I was often more receptive to him than to my mother. Recently, I have discovered that I may have incurred even more damage than I had realized. However, I am now in a space where I can use my voice to give a firm "No" when I feel that I am being used, manipulated, or controlled. The power of no is so essential; creating boundaries is another form of self-love. I am hoping to get to a place where there is something about me that says: "You can't talk to me or treat me any old kind of way and expect it to be acceptable or permissible. Just because I present with sweet and caring energy does not mean that you have a license to mistreat me."

I have always been a strong Black woman. Still, I recall having to use my voice in situations where I might have been dominated, violated, or victimized, even in professional settings. I had to learn that being sweet and kind is not enough. The answer to this dilemma is no. The world can sometimes mistake a woman's laid-back demeanor for passiveness and mistake her for a pushover. I used to go into shock when I was disrespected; I would be locked-jawed when it came to speaking up and saying: "This is not right. Stop this. I do not like this," or "I do not want to talk." In the end, I learned that it was OK to use my voice to disagree vocally. Many abused children are programmed to remain silent when they cannot speak or vocalize their deep hurt. This response is part of their trauma. Control has a long-lasting impact if we do not do the work needed to become healthy and whole again. When we love ourselves, that positive light begins to shine through powerfully, and we begin to attract what we are. Everything vibrates in our part of the spectrum. I have so much to be thankful for. As a youngster, I walked around, feeling dismal, filled with gloom and doom. As I came of age, my hormones calmed down, and Jehovah Rapha sent His healing balm to fill up the empty spaces that were left behind after the trauma and pain. "God will turn our mourning into dancing" (Psalm 30:11) and "give us the garment of praise in exchange for the spirit of heaviness" (Isaiah 61:3)

When I had my son almost twenty years ago, I realized that I had no time to be self-centered or focused on my own pain. Two years before having him, I made dietary changes and noticed that I no longer cried three times a week. I believe this resulted from a combination of things: first, seeking my deliverance at GRT; second, radically changing my diet to a semi-vegetarian diet in 1997; and third, giving birth to and raising my child. I am so proud of my son; he is an aspiring Hip Hop artist who has made some fantastic strides in pursuing his career as a producer, songwriter, and performer. I am happy to say that my son is also doing well in his other pursuits. He has faced many obstacles and is learning the skills that he needs to navigate this world. I am proud to say that my son has become a praying man and is learning to depend on the God that lives inside of him. I am blessed and honored to be his mother, and he is the fruit of my labor.

"When love calls us, we better answer" was an old song by the R&B group *Atlantic Starr* back in the early 1980s. When we love God and love where He has called us to, we should willfully answer the call and go. We should have a willful heart and an optimistic attitude, as the prophet Isaiah did (Isaiah 6:8), when he said, "Here am I, send me." Are we willing to go when love calls us to a new assignment, a new town, a new space, or the next chapter of our lives? Are we willing to take that journey into the unknown? Will we end up in the abyss or trust God wholeheartedly to provide the things He has promised us on earth and in eternity? We have a choice to make: we can choose to take the familiar path that we want or take the "road less traveled," moving forward onto the beautiful and glorious path that God has destined for us. We detour, get sidetracked, become arrogant, think that we know what is best for us better than our Heavenly Father does, and we forsake being directed by love. The Bible says, "My dear friends, let us love one another since love is from God and everyone who loves is a child of God and knows God. Whoever fails to love does not know God, because God is love" (I John 4:7-8). If we ever needed a measuring stick to define what love is clearly, we should use the following definition: "Love is patient and kind. Love is not jealous or boastful or proud or rude. It does not demand its own way. It is not irritable, and it keeps no record of being wronged. It does not rejoice about injustice but rejoices whenever the truth wins out. Love never gives up, never loses faith, is always hopeful, and endures through every circumstance" (1 Corinthians 13:4-7).

The previous scripture defines what love is—perfect love. If these aspects of love are missing in our relationships, we must ask whether we are truly loving. Perhaps it's time to re-evaluate and unlearn our ideas of love, which allowed us to pass down distortions and a flawed concept simply because we did not know what love was supposed to be. We have forsaken the simplicity of the divine instruction manual that was always there to guide each one of us into true, pure, and lasting love.

Scriptural Nugget: 1 Corinthians 13:4-8 New Living Translation

"Love is patient and kind. Love is not jealous or boastful or proud or rude. It does not demand its own way. It is not irritable, and it keeps no record of being wronged. It does not rejoice about injustice but rejoices whenever the truth wins out. Love never gives up, never loses faith, is always hopeful, and endures through every circumstance. Prophecy and speaking in unknown languages and special knowledge will become useless. But love will last forever!"

Acknowledgments

I would like to honor the memory of my dear mother, who was a class act even in her vulnerabilities, dysfunction, flaws, and mistakes. I forgive you for simply not knowing, and I am thankful for what you did know. Our talks were priceless, and you taught me so much. Suppose smartphone devices had been popular just a few years before you left. In that case, we could have recorded your kitchen lectures, and you would have made millions of dollars as a conference speaker, rivaling Joyce Meyer in your delivery, as we once joked. I miss you, and I love you always. Daddy, I miss your strength, your intelligence, your extensive vocabulary, your calm, cool humor tinged with sarcasm, your sensitivity, your sound logic, and your strong, firm hugs. I did not think I would make it when you left me, but I am still here and able to smile.

To both grandmothers, I honor you both. To my maternal grandmother, Gloria, who raised me, I thank you for being a classy woman who taught me how to live with dignity, class, and elegance and also showing me on your dying day how to draw your last breath with beauty and grace. You were a diva until the end, granny, and I miss you. To my paternal grandmother, I am thankful to have inherited your tenacity, your academic acumen, and your determination to thrive and survive. To my great-grandmother, I thank you for being present during my formative years and taking care of me. I miss you and thank you for being a wise counselor to all who came in contact with you.

To Aunt Angela, I thank God for you. I am so fortunate to have you in my life in this place and time. I wish we could have met much sooner, but God knows best, and I trust His timing. I thank God for all the women, aunts, uncles, spiritual mothers, spiritual fathers, and all who had a hand in shaping and developing me into the woman I am today. I thank my son, Ayinde, for radically shifting me into purpose. You were and are my biggest motivator, pushing me to become the best mother I could and can be. Thank you for choosing me to be your mother. God, I thank you for each and every moment that you've given me, even when I was bewildered by life. I thank you for your grace, your mercy, your love, and your forgiveness. God, you are a good, good Father, and your plans are perfect. I love you, Lord! I thank you for trying me once again. Amen.

www.ingramcontent.com/pod-product-compliance
Lightning Source LLC
LaVergne TN
LVHW041629070426
835507LV00008B/521